GENE

Effective Lawyering

Effective Lawyering

A Checklist Approach
to Legal Writing
and Oral Argument

Austen L. Parrish
IRWIN R. BUCHALTER PROFESSOR OF LAW
DIRECTOR, VANCOUVER SUMMER LAW PROGRAM
SOUTHWESTERN LAW SCHOOL

Dennis T. Yokoyama
PAUL E. TREUSCH PROFESSOR OF LAW
SOUTHWESTERN LAW SCHOOL

CAROLINA ACADEMIC PRESS
Durham, North Carolina

Library of Congress Cataloging-in-Publication Data

Parrish, Austen L.
  Effective lawyering : a checklist approach to legal writing and oral
argument / by Austen L. Parrish, Dennis T. Yokoyama.
    p. cm.
  Includes bibliographical references and index.
  ISBN-13: 978-1-59460-348-8 (alk. paper)
  ISBN-10: 1-59460-348-0 (alk. paper)
  1. Legal composition. 2. Law--United States--Methodology. 3.
Oral pleading--United States. 4. Briefs--United States. I.
Yokoyama, Dennis T. II. Title.

  KF250.P37 2007
  808'.06634--dc22

                                              2007008478

CAROLINA ACADEMIC PRESS
700 Kent Street
Durham, North Carolina 27701
Telephone (919) 489-7486
Fax (919) 493-5668
www.cap-press.com

Printed in the United States of America

for Leslie, Natalie, and Amelie
AP

for Janis and Denise
DY

Summary of Contents

Contents

Acknowledgments

We are grateful to those who read and commented on this book during its many drafts, and for the support of Southwestern Law School and our colleagues in the Legal Analysis, Writing and Skills Program. Special thanks to Ron Aronovsky, Anahid Gharakhanian, Michael Frost, Russell Miller, Lillian Aponte Miranda, Ashley Parrish, Byron Stier, Tara Walters, and Janis Yokoyama for their good ideas and encouragement. We are also indebted to Joshua Kane and John Stephenson for their research assistance. Finally, we thank our students from whom we have learned much.

About the Authors

Austen L. Parrish: Professor Parrish is the Irwin R. Buchalter Professor of Law at Southwestern Law School, where he has taught courses in legal writing and appellate advocacy, including Legal Process, Introduction to Legal Writing, and Legal Research and Writing. He currently teaches Civil Pretrial Practice, an advanced writing and skills seminar, as well as Civil Procedure, Federal Courts, and International Environmental Law. Professor Parrish earned his B.A. from the University of Washington, in Seattle, and was a Harlan Fiske Stone Scholar at Columbia Law School. During law school, Professor Parrish served as a Managing Editor of the Columbia Journal of Transnational Law and a student editor for the Columbia Journal of European Law.

From 1997–2002, Professor Parrish was an attorney in the Litigation Department of O'Melveny & Myers in Los Angeles. In 2002, he joined the Southwestern Faculty, and in 2003 was appointed the Director of Southwestern's Summer Law Program in Vancouver, B.C., Canada. He is a faculty advisor to the Southwestern Journal of Law and Trade in the Americas, and has received awards for his work with Southwestern's Moot Court Honors Program. In 2007, he was honored with Southwestern's Excellence in Teaching Award.

Dennis T. Yokoyama: Professor Yokoyama is the Paul E. Treusch professor of law at Southwestern Law School where he has taught Civil Procedure, Remedies, Legal Process, Introduction to Legal Writing, and Legal Research and Writing. Professor Yokoyama earned his B.A. from the University of California, Los Angeles, his M.S. in Clinical Psychology (Family Therapy) from California State University, Los Angeles, and his J.D. from Loyola Law School in Los Angeles, where he was Order of the Coif. During law school, Professor Yokoyama served as a staff member and articles editor for the Entertainment Law Journal.

Professor Yokoyama began his legal career at the law firm of Paul, Hastings, Janofsky & Walker in Los Angeles, where he worked as an associate with the firm's environmental and commercial litigation practice group. In 1992, Professor Yokoyama joined Southwestern's legal writing faculty, and, from 1995–2007 served as Director of the Legal Research and Writing Program. In 2000, he was honored with Southwestern's Excellence in Teaching Award.

Introduction

This book takes a unique approach to legal writing and oral advocacy. Many excellent legal writing books exhaustively detail how to write effectively. Those books—many of which are several hundred pages long, and contain numerous examples and exercises—meticulously explain the dos and don'ts of effective advocacy. This is not one of those books. This book assumes the reader has learned or is learning the basics of legal writing, and at most needs only reminding of what they are. It also assumes that most practitioners (and, for that matter, law students) have neither the time, nor the inclination, to read a lengthy discussion of all the subtleties of legal method. Busy lawyers and law students need a book that gets to the point quickly—a book that will be useful even if they only have time to skim it.

For these reasons, we have designed this book to be a concise, easy-to-use reference—not a book to be read cover to cover. We intend it to provide concrete advice, and to serve as a day-to-day reference. Because many people find it difficult to improve their legal writing, the book has adopted a methodical approach. In our experience, practitioners and students alike can improve their advocacy by following carefully crafted checklists. Checklists force writers to focus on specific problems and help them improve incrementally and systematically. The checklists in this book have evolved from our experiences as former litigators and professors of legal writing.

So who should use this book? This book is suited for busy attorneys and law students of all stripes. The book concisely describes useful, yet often neglected, writing techniques. It has pithy discussions of: (1) ways to avoid recurring, yet frequently overlooked, writing problems; (2) sensible approaches to writing common legal documents; and (3) methods for preparing an oral argument. In addition, it provides the reader with a series of checklists to turn to when undertaking a writing project or preparing for oral argument. In sum, this book, by itself, is not for the novice who requires a comprehensive guide, although the book can be used to supplement more exhaustive texts. Nor is it for the sophisticated writing expert, looking for nuanced discussions about topics not commonly covered in legal writing books. But it is for practitioners and students who want to be refreshed on the fundamentals of effective lawyering.

Effective Lawyering

Chapter 1

Techniques for Effective Legal Writing

Surprisingly, given how often they write and the high stakes involved, attorneys often write terribly. Even terrible writing, however, can contain sound argument. The problem is that poor organization, convoluted sentences, and ineffective references to authority obscure otherwise persuasive and insightful analysis.

What follows are concrete ways for you to improve your writing. This chapter describes how to: (1) write effective paragraphs; (2) write effective sentences; (3) steer clear of attorney pet-peeves; (4) avoid common grammatical errors; (5) use authority effectively; and (6) format your legal documents. These techniques apply to all the types of legal writing discussed in this book in later chapters: trial court briefs, appellate court briefs, interoffice memoranda, letters, and academic writing.

Writing Effective Paragraphs

Very few people read legal writing only for pleasure; readers expect you to make your point clearly and concisely so that they can take appropriate action. To do this, you must write coherent paragraphs that connect together logically. Here are six ways to accomplish that goal.

3

A. Write Clear Topic Sentences

For the sake of unity and cohesiveness, each paragraph should have an informative topic sentence. The topic sentence should announce the paragraph's purpose or main point. In brief writing, framing the topic sentence as a conclusion is often best. In a brief, if you write every topic sentence properly, a court should be able to read just the first sentence of each paragraph and understand your argument.

B. Roadmap and Signpost Your Arguments

Roadmaps—sometimes referred to as thesis paragraphs—are introductory paragraphs that provide an overview of the analysis or arguments to come. Use roadmaps to enhance readability and to orient the reader to the structure of the analysis. Good writers will also, at times, explicitly signpost the major points of their argument. Example: "This Court should grant the requested relief for three reasons. First.... Second.... Third...."

C. Link Your Paragraphs

You should link paragraphs to one another with transition words or phrases. Do not leave the reader wondering "how did I get here?" To connect paragraphs, use hook words (e.g., *this, that, these, those*), transitions (e.g., *additionally, also, conversely, similarly, therefore*), or echo/bridging links (repeating key words, phrases, or ideas mentioned in the preceding paragraph).

D. Link Your Sentences

Not only should you link your paragraphs, you also should link sentences within the paragraph. Each sentence should logically lead to the next. Connecting your sentences with hook words, transitions, or echo links will make your writing more cohesive.

E. Make Only One Main Point

Each paragraph should focus on one main point. An effective topic sentence will help you draft a paragraph that is coherent and that focuses on one point. Make sure that every sentence in a paragraph relates to the topic sentence. Remove details in the paragraph that are extraneous to the paragraph's topic sentence.

F. Revise Overly Short or Long Paragraphs

Ordinarily, legal documents should not have one-sentence paragraphs. Properly fleshing out a point almost always requires two or more sentences. In addition, as a matter of style, you generally should have at least one paragraph break in a double-spaced typed page. If a single paragraph fills the entire page, break up the paragraph into two or more paragraphs. A paragraph exceeding one page presents a daunting task for the reader.

* * * * *

> "[The brief writer must be immersed] in the chaos of detail and bring order to it by organizing—and I cannot stress that term enough—by organizing, organizing, and organizing...."
>
> —Chief Justice William Rehnquist
> (quoted in Scott Wood, Practical Persuasion:
> A Writing Workshop 9 (2002)).

Writing Effective Sentences

Effective legal writers employ concrete language that conveys complex ideas concisely and plainly. They also eliminate superfluous words so that their writing is lean, clear, and direct. The following suggestions will help you write better sentences.

A. Write Short Sentences

As much as any other factor, sentence length determines readability. Your sentences should average 20–25 words. All sentences, however, should not be the same length. Varying the length of your sentences will improve readability and help avoid monotony. You do not have to count words to spot long sentences. If a sentence is three lines or more, consider trimming it or breaking it up into two or more sentences.

"My advice to brief writers is to be brief. Say what you have to say in reasonably short declarative sentences powered by nouns and verbs. If a sentence has more than twenty words, it usually needs to be redrafted."

—Hon. Arthur Gilbert, Presiding Justice, California Court of Appeal (quoted in Bryan A. Garner, *Judges on Briefing: A National Survey*, 8 Scribes J. Legal Writing 1, 9 (2001–2002)).

B. Prefer the Active Voice

Active voice focuses the reader on the actor, not the object being acted on. The basic structure of an active sentence is: actor → action → object. You can detect passive voice by looking for a *be*-verb (e.g., *is, are, was,* or *were*) followed by a past participle (usually a verb ending in-*ed)* and then often by a conjunction (e.g., *by, for, with,* etc.). Passive voice has its uses, of course. Passive voice is appropriate when you wish to hide the actor, the actor is unimportant, or you wish to focus on the object of the action and the reader knows the actor's identity. Yet active voice is usually preferable to passive voice because it: (1) is economical, requiring less words; (2) makes the writing more direct, crisp, and lively; and (3) avoids ambiguity. To make a sentence active, focus first on the actor, then the action, and finally the object. Example: "The contract was signed by Jim." → "Jim signed the contract."

C. Consider Possessives

Tighten your writing and eliminate unnecessary words by converting some *of* phrases to possessives. Example: "The obligations of Jane" → "Jane's obligations".

D. Keep the Subject and Verb Together

To improve clarity, as a general rule, keep a sentence's subject and verb together. Separating a sentence's subject and verb with intervening clauses makes the sentence difficult to understand. Starting your sentences with a subject followed immediately by a verb also improves readability and eliminates passive voice. Example: "The issue whether to vote for the bill was considered by the Senator." → "The <u>Senator</u> <u>considered</u> whether to vote for the bill."
      Subject   Verb

E. Remove Wordy Constructions

Expletive constructions, such as *there is, there are, it is,* or *it was,* are wordy and can be ambiguous. You often can structure your sentences to avoid them. Example: "There are three reasons why the court should deny this motion." → "The court should deny this motion for three reasons."

> *"Omit needless words! Omit needless words! Omit needless words!"*
>
> —William Strunk Jr. & E.B. White, The Elements Of Style
> xv (4th ed. 2000).

F. Resist Throat Clearing

Attorneys habitually use long-winded preambles—called throat clearers—to begin sentences. Common throat clearers include: *It is important to note that ... ; It must, of course, be remembered that ... ;* and *Suffice it to say.*... Omit throat clearers. They are wordy, obscure the sentence's main point, and add little if anything to the sentence's meaning.

G. Use Verbs, Not Nominalizations

Nominalizations are nouns created from verbs and adjectives. You can spot many nominalizations by looking for noun endings such as *-ant*, *-ancy*, *-ence*, *-ency*, *-ity*, *-ion*, or *-ment*. Nominalizations weigh down your writing by making your sentences wordy and frequently passive. Instead of nominalizations, use their base verbs:

Examples:

Wordy Nominalization	*Verb*
conduct an examination of	examine
contains a discussion of	discusses
make a recommendation	recommend
reached an agreement	agreed
submit an application	apply

Nominalizations do have their uses. Nominalizations are useful as shorthand to identify an act previously described and to link two sentences. Example: "The dean decided to give faculty only a one percent raise. This *decision* [nominalization of *to decide*] caused the faculty to revolt."

> "To express ... life and motion, a writer must use verbs—action words.... If you use nominalizations instead of base verbs, surplus words begin to swarm like gnats."
>
> —RICHARD C. WYDICK,
> PLAIN ENGLISH FOR LAWYERS 23 (5th ed. 2005).

H. Be Positive

Prefer affirmative sentences. Search for and consider replacing phrases like *did not* and *do not* with positive constructions. Negative sentences often lack force and can be confusing, wordy, and ambiguous. Never use double negatives.

Examples:

Negatives/Double Negatives	*Replacement*
not unlikely	likely

not impossible	possible
not unlike	similar
not able	unable
does not have	lacks

I. Avoid Abbreviations, Initialisms, and Defined Terms

Be careful in using acronyms, abbreviations, initialisms, or defined terms. They can make your writing hard to follow. You should only use initials when the term is familiar to most readers (e.g., BMW, IBM, or SEC). Do not abbreviate parties' names using initials. Example: Refer to Mercedes-Benz Club of America as *Mercedes* or *the Club*, not as *MBCA*.

* * * * *

Avoiding Attorney Pet Peeves

All attorneys have their pet peeves when it comes to legal writing: common errors that make experienced writers cringe. Here are some that you should avoid.

A. Omit Overused Adverbs and Adjectives

Avoid overused adverbs, such as *clearly, obviously, totally, plainly,* and *manifestly*. This sort of adverb indicates an absoluteness that does little to bolster your argument or to persuade your reader. These types of adverbs sometimes actually highlight an argument's weakness. *Clearly* is the most overused adverb of all. Avoid using it. If something were clear, you would not have to argue for it. Some adjectives also add nothing but empty baggage to your writing. Use adjectives to add precision, but be cautious of words used for emphasis. The word *very*, for example, is overused. Leave it out of your sentence, unless it changes the sentence's meaning.

B. Never Write in Legalese—Use Plain English

Resist the temptation to sound "lawyerly" without saying anything meaningful. Avoid phrases such as *said, such, aforementioned, wheretofore, heretofore, to wit*, as well as unnecessary Latinisms. Legalese is a telltale sign of either an inexperienced lawyer trying to sound erudite, or a lawyer hopelessly lost in ancient conventions. The cure? Use plain English.

Examples:

Legalese	*Plain English*
aforesaid	before, this
forthwith	immediately
hereinabove	above
heretofore	before
inasmuch as	because, since
in the event that	if

Writing in plain English does not mean using slang or colloquial language. As with legalese, slang is inappropriate for formal legal writing. Writing in plain English means using the everyday word rather than the ornate or obscure one.

> "[I]n general it is the second-rate intellect that cultivates a pretentious vocabulary and a solemn and portentous style."
>
> —Hon. Richard A. Posner, 7th Cir. Court of Appeals (quoted in BRYAN A. GARNER, THE RED BOOK 162 (2002)).

C. Delete *In Order To*

Avoid using the phrase *in order to*, the *in order* is superfluous. Delete *in order* and use simply *to*. Example: "In order to win this case...." → "To win this case...."

D. Delete *The Fact That*

Rarely is there a reason to use phrases with the words *the fact that*. Delete them.

Examples:

Wordy Phrase	*Replacement*
because of the fact that	because
despite the fact that	although
due to the fact that	because
in light of the fact that	in light of

> *"I abhor, loathe and despise these long discourses, and agree with Carducci the Italian poet who died some years ago that a man who takes half a page to say what can be said in a sentence will be damned."*
>
> —Oliver Wendell Holmes, Jr., Letter to Frederick Pollock,
> June 1, 1917, in Mark DeWolfe Howe, ed.
> HOLMES-POLLOCK LETTERS 1:245 (1941) (quoted in
> FRED R. SHAPIRO, THE OXFORD DICTIONARY OF
> AMERICAN LEGAL QUOTATIONS 289 (1993)).

E. Eliminate Inflammatory Language

Your writing will possess greater force if you avoid using adjectives such as *outrageous, shocking,* or *vexatious* to describe an opponent's conduct, or even worse an opponent. Overblown rhetoric will undermine your credibility and weaken the force of your arguments. Instead of saying that your opponent is *outrageous*, describe what your opponent has done. Show, don't tell.

F. Remove Parenthetical Numerals

Attorneys have an annoying habit of spelling out numbers and then including a parenthetical with a numeral (e.g., "I ate two (2) apples, three (3) oranges, and four (4) pears."). The habit is irritating, pointless, and makes the sentence more difficult to read. Do not do it. When you write "*two*," you can be confident that the reader knows what you mean.

G. Avoid Worn-Out Metaphors and Clichés

Metaphors can be used effectively to create potent imagery. All too often, however, attorneys overuse metaphors that have become tired clichés. Even worse, sometimes metaphors or idioms are used incorrectly (e.g., "tow the line" instead of "toe the line"). The problem with overused metaphors and clichés is that they lack impact. You use them at the expense of individuality and precision. Examples: "swan song," "woven into the fabric of society," "wearing rose-colored glasses," "the wheels of justice grind," "doors slammed shut."

* * * * *

Grammar Tips

Grammar is important for attorneys because most people (especially clients and judges) expect grammatical writing. This does not mean, however, that you should memorize lists of all the technical grammar terms. Instead, practitioners should have a usage guide at hand that they can refer to for finding reliable answers to grammar questions.[1] The following identifies some basic grammar or usage mistakes that attorneys commonly make.

A. *That* and *Which*

Many writers confuse how to use *that* and *which*. The distinction between the two, however, is straightforward. A comma does not precede *that*. *That* should introduce a restrictive/dependent clause

---

1. Two particularly good grammar guides that also include legal style suggestions are: (1) ANNE ENQUIST & LAUREL CURRIE OATES, JUST WRITING: GRAMMAR, PUNCTUATION, AND STYLE FOR THE LEGAL WRITER (2d ed. 2005); and (2) BRYAN A. GARNER, THE REDBOOK: A MANUAL ON LEGAL STYLE (2d ed. 2006).

(i.e., a clause that is essential to the sentence's meaning). A comma usually precedes *which* to introduce a nonrestrictive/independent clause (i.e., a clause that is unnecessary to the sentence's meaning).

B. Parallelism

Parallelism is a grammatical requirement that ideas or elements of a sentence are presented in the same form. Verb tenses, pronouns, and articles must match the subject in sentences. When ordering a list, you should match the list's elements grammatically. You should match adjectives with adjectives, adverbs with adverbs, nouns with nouns, and so on. Lack of parallelism can confuse the reader. Example: "The judge wanted to read the briefs, research law, and to write the decision." → "The judge wanted to read the briefs, research the law, and write the decision."

C. Subject-Verb Agreement

A subject must agree with its verb. If a subject is singular, the verb must also be singular (e.g., "The Appell*ant* *is* mistaken."). Plural subjects must have plural verbs (e.g., "The Appell*ants* *are* mistaken.").

Keep in mind the following rules: First, multiple subjects usually require a plural verb (e.g., "John and Jane *are* friends."). Second, singular subjects joined by *or* or *nor* usually take singular verbs (e.g., "Neither John nor Jane *is* upset"). Third, collective nouns—such as a jury or appellate court—usually require singular verbs (e.g., "This Court *has* ruled"; "The jury *has* decided"). The words *anybody, everyone, each,* or *every* are singular pronouns that require singular verbs. These rules apply even when intervening phrases separate the subject from its verb.

> *"We use correct grammar to communicate clearly. Don't let the traditional rules of grammar and its incomprehensible terms (such as pluperfect or subjunctive) intimidate you. You do not need to know the names of the parts of speech to be a good writer, just as you do not need to know all the parts of a microwave oven to be a good cook."*
>
> —Deborah E. Bouchoux, Aspen Handbook for Legal Writers:
> A Practical Reference 4 (2005).

D. Contractions/Possessive Pronouns

In legal writing, you should avoid using contractions; they are often deemed too informal. Instead, write out the contraction (e.g., it's—it is; can't—can not; don't—do not). Also, be careful not to confuse contractions with possessives. *It's*, *there's*, and *who's* are contractions. *Its*, *theirs*, and *whose* are possessive pronouns.

E. Elegant Variation

A writer engages in elegant variation by using multiple terms to identify someone or something. Be careful before using elegant variation in legal writing. Elegant variation may unintentionally lead the reader to assume that you have used the different word for a substantive, rather than a stylistic, reason. Once you have labeled a party, be certain that you use the same label consistently. An example: if your brief first refers to the plaintiff as *Smith*, every later reference to the plaintiff should be to *Smith*, not to *plaintiff* or *Jane* (her first name), or to *Ms. Smith*.

F. Gender-Neutral Language

Modern legal writers avoid using gender-specific forms, unless writing about something that concerns only one gender. You often can avoid gender-specific language (e.g., *he* or *she*) by changing singular nouns to plural nouns. Alternatively, many sentences can be rewritten so that: (1) pronouns are not used; or (2) indefinite pronouns (e.g., *one*) are utilized instead. Avoid using the awkward and distracting phrases *he/she* or *s/he*. Alternating between *he* and *she* is similarly confusing and imprecise, and therefore is not recommended.

G. Split Infinitives

A split infinitive exists when an adverb is placed between *to* and the verb form (e.g., "to clearly establish"). A split infinitive is not a grammatical error. But many senior attorneys and judges still view it as an error. Sound practice then is to follow the general rule against splitting infinitives, unless doing so leads to an awkward phrasing.

* * * * *

> *"Every good literary craftsman splits his infinitives when the sense demands it. I call for the immediate dismissal of the pedant on your staff [who chases split infinitives]. It is of no consequence whether he decides to go quickly or to quickly go."*
>
> —George Bernard Shaw (quoted in Wilson Follett, Modern American Usage 313 (1966)).

Using Authority Effectively

Attorneys often do not use authority as they should. What follows are not citation rules, but tips on how to use authority effectively.

A. Quote Properly

A few rules govern the use of quotations. First, you should rarely, if ever, use lengthy block quotations. Most readers either skim or skip block quotes. A better practice is to weave portions of the quotation into your own text. Second, if you must use a block quotation, keep the quote short. Include only the essential information. Third, in general, you should only use quotations when they express an idea in a particularly eloquent way, or place the reader in touch with the thinking of the court (e.g., the quote is a concise, plain statement of a holding) or other authority.

B. Remove String Citations

Do not cite to multiple cases when citing to one controlling case will do. A long list of cites interrupts the flow of the text, and, ironically, often gives the appearance that none of the cites are on point. String citations are generally appropriate only in the rare instance when the law is unclear in your jurisdiction and you wish to show that the weight of authority from other jurisdictions favors your position.

C. Remove Mid-Sentence Citations

Think carefully before you cite to authority in the middle of a sentence. Although often done, embedding a citation forces a reader to "jump" between text and citation, hindering readability. Placing the citation at the end of the sentence is usually the better practice.

D. Use Pinpoint Citations

Always cite your point to the precise page number from the authority you rely on. These are known as pinpoint or jump cites.

E. Paraphrase and Cite Accurately

Too many attorneys fail to cite correctly in both substance and form. Your paraphrasing should accurately convey the substance of your source material, not only for ethical reasons, but because your credibility is on the line. Even one misstatement of the law, or an inaccurate description of a holding, can compromise the credibility of your entire argument.

F. Resist Footnoting

Writing experts disagree as to the wisdom of placing citations in footnotes when writing court briefs, letters, or legal memoranda. Although some experts have urged their use, many judges still dislike the practice. Early in your career, the best practice is to follow what senior attorneys in your office, or the judges you are before, prefer. For legal briefs, do not place anything of significance or substance in a footnote. If you do use footnotes, use them sparingly to make ancillary points.

* * * * *

> "Footnotes detract from readability. Encountering a footnote is like going downstairs to answer the door while making love.... 'If footnotes were a rational form of communication, Darwinian selection would have resulted in the eyes being set vertically....'"
>
> —Judge Mark R. Painter, *Legal Writing 201: 30 Tips to Improve Readability in Briefs and Legal Documents Or, How to Write for Judges, Not Like Judges*, MONT. LAW., Apr. 2006, at 9 (quoting Mikva, *Goodbye to Footnotes*, 56 U. COL. L. REV. 647, 648 (1985)).

Formatting with Style

Many lawyers underestimate the importance of a professional-looking brief, memorandum, or letter. Using a clear format—while following local court rules or law office custom—is essential for readability and, accordingly, persuasiveness. A cramped, poorly designed legal document undermines the effectiveness of even the strongest written advocacy. Judges and senior attorneys often instinctively equate sloppy-looking documents with sloppy lawyering.

A. Typeface

Use a serifed typeface, like Times New Roman, Century, or Palatino, in an easy-to-read size (12 point or larger). Fonts like Courier or Arial, which are not serifed, are harder to read, and are generally considered less professional looking. Never use a decorative type, such as Comic Sans. You should use the same typeface throughout a legal document. Footnotes, unless court rules require otherwise, should be deemphasized by formatting them in a slightly smaller font (e.g., 11 point Times New Roman).

> *"Word processors have changed lawyers' work environment tremendously … [T]hey have made a designer out of every user. Even following the same set of court rules and writing the same kind of document, two lawyers—one knowledgeable in document design and one not—can end up with documents that look quite different: one can be pleasant-looking, the other offputting."*
>
> —Bryan A. Garner, The Redbook:
> A Manual on Legal Style 77 (2006).

B. Headings

Whether in briefs or memoranda, distinguish your headings from your text by single-spacing and bolding them. Also, indent subheadings. One effective style is to format your centered headings in bold/all caps (so long as the heading is relatively short), your main headings in bold/title case, and your subheadings in bold/sentence case. Example:

HEADING

I. Main Headings In Title Case And Bold

   A. Subheadings in sentence case and bold

Whatever format you use, make sure that your headings and sub-headings are formatted consistently.

C. Justification

The easiest-to-read document is one where the text is flush left to produce a jagged right margin. Do not fully justify your text (unless court rules require otherwise), as it will create uneven spacing problems that make the text harder to read. Right justification will also cause problems with your citation spacing. Fully justified text is common in professionally printed documents, where professional typesetters can eliminate the uneven spacing.

D. Bold, Italics, and Underline

With the exception of their use in headings, you should use formatted fonts (such as bold, italics, and underlining) sparingly. Too often attorneys, for emphasis, will bold, underline, or italicize consecutive sentences or even paragraphs. This is counterproductive: it distracts the reader and can weaken the argument. Bold and italics should be rarely and selectively used to emphasize only key words or short phrases. Avoid underlining, except in very rare instances and do not write long headings in all-capital letters. Underlined text and text in ALL CAPS— conventions leftover from the days of typewriters—are difficult to read.

E. Bullets

Bullet points are underused in legal documents. Bullets can effectively emphasize key factual or legal points. A few things to keep in mind when using them:

- bullets should follow a sentence ending with a colon, and should be block indented with a hanging indent;
- generally begin your bullet points with a lower case letter and end with a semi-colon after each bullet but the last, which should end with a period; and

- if you begin each bullet with a capital letter, make sure each bullet point is a complete sentence and then end each bullet with a period.

Bullets often look best when single-spaced—but you should double-space between each bullet.

F. Orphaned and Widowed Text

Be careful to avoid orphaning or widowing text. You orphan text when you begin a page with the last line of the previous page's paragraph. You widow text when you end a page with the first line of a new paragraph. Orphaned and widowed text looks unprofessional, and makes the document more difficult to read. This is particularly true with widowed text, which separates the topic sentence from the body of the paragraph. The same rules apply for headings and subheadings. Do not strand headings from paragraph text, or split a heading so that part of the heading appears on one page, and the remainder on the next. Dealing with orphaned and widowed text generally comes in the last stage of editing.

* * * * *

Effective Writing Checklist

Use the following checklist for any legal document—be it a brief, letter, memorandum, or article—to improve systematically your writing style.

Step 1: Revise, Tighten, and Clarify Your Paragraphs

Review each paragraph, with the following in mind:

❏ Does each paragraph begin with a strong topic sentence that captures the paragraph's main point (stated as a conclusion, if used in persuasive writing)?

❏ Have you used signposts, when appropriate, to show where the argument or discussion is leading (First.... Second.... Third....)?

❏ Does each paragraph convey one, and only one, main point?

❏ Are your paragraphs the appropriate length? Be certain you have no one-sentence paragraphs or a paragraph filling more than a page.

❏ Are your paragraphs connected? Have you used hook words, transitions, or echo links to connect the paragraphs?

Step 2: Revise, Tighten, and Clarify Your Sentences

Next, focus on each sentence of each paragraph. Edit and revise word-by-word, phrase-by-phrase, asking yourself:

❏ Sentence Length: Are your sentences, on average, 20-25 words or less (or three lines or shorter)? Have you varied the length of your sentences: some short, some long?

❏ Active Voice: Do you have any *be*-verbs followed by a word ending in *-ed* and then the word *by*? Have you used active voice, unless you have a good reason for using passive voice?

❏ Possessives: Can you convert any *of* phrases to possessives?

❏ Is the subject and verb in each sentence close together?

❏ Have you spotted all unnecessary nominalizations and rewritten them as active verbs?

❏ Have you eliminated wordy constructions (often starting with *there is, there are, it is,* or *it was*) or throat clearers?

❏ Have you framed your sentences affirmatively, rather than negatively? Have you rewritten double negatives?

❏ Have you avoided using abbreviations, acronyms, or defined terms, except when necessary and absolutely clear?

Step 3: Remove Writing Blunders

In Step 3, you want to review systematically each paragraph again. This time, be sure to remove the most annoying writing blunders.

❏ Have you removed legalese, and used plain English?

❏ Have you avoided using adverbs, such as *totally, manifestly, plainly, clearly,* or *obviously*? Have you avoided unnecessarily using the word *very*?

❏ Have you deleted any instance where you have unnecessarily used *in order to* or *the fact that*?

❏ Have you refrained from using inflammatory language, purple prose, or overblown rhetoric?

❏ Have you removed parenthetical numerals?

❏ Have you avoided clichés and worn-out metaphors?

Step 4: Avoid Common Grammar Mistakes

Next review each sentence to remove any common grammatical errors.

❏ Have you correctly used *that* and *which*? Are all *which*s introducing independent clauses preceded by a comma?

❏ Do your lists use parallel grammatical structure?

❑ Do all your subjects agree with their verbs?

❑ Have you eliminated contractions?

❑ Have you used gender-neutral language?

❑ Have you been consistent in how you refer to parties, avoiding elegant variation?

❑ Have you corrected any unnecessary split infinitives?

Step 5: Use Authority Effectively

In Step 5, review all citations in your document asking yourself:

❑ Have you avoided block quotes? When you have used a block quote, does it contain only essential information?

❑ Have you removed unnecessary string citations? Is each citation there for a precise reason?

❑ Have you avoided citing in mid-sentence? Are all citations at the end of the sentence?

❑ Does each citation to authority have a pinpoint/jump cite?

❑ Is each citation accurate? Have you followed correct citation rules for your jurisdiction? Is each statement of the law accurate?

❑ Have you resisted footnoting? When you do footnote, have you limited the footnote to citing to authority or making an ancillary point? If anything significant or substantive appears in the footnote, move it up to the text.

Step 6: Appropriately Format and Design Your Document

Finally review the entire document. Is it aesthetically pleasing? Does it look professional? Ask yourself the following:

❑ Have you followed all local court rules and law office customs?

❑ Have you used a serifed typeface (do not use courier, arial, and decorative fonts)?

❏ Have you used the same typeface throughout the document?

❏ Are your headings separated from the text?

❏ Are your headings easy to distinguish from the text, because they are either bolded or italicized?

❏ Is your document justification flush left, producing a jagged right margin?

❏ Have you avoided underlining or using ALL CAPS for long headings?

❏ Have you used bold or italics in the text sparingly to emphasize only key words, or short phrases?

❏ Can you use bullets to emphasize key factual or legal points?

Chapter 2

Trial Court Briefs

Judges are busy people. Like attorneys, judges are juggling a large and ever-growing number of cases. They do not have time to wade through wordy, impenetrable, and convoluted briefs. Like other readers, judges can get confused, frustrated, and even angered by poor writing.

A major part of a litigator's task is to make the judge's job as easy as possible. Too often, however, briefs—even those from seasoned litigators—are difficult to read and hard to follow. The result is predictable. A lawyer who submits a poorly written brief has made it less likely that the court will rule favorably for that lawyer's client. Good briefs, on the other hand, are strong pieces of written advocacy— clear, crisp, and easy to follow. While a good brief is no guarantee of success, it may tip the scales in that side's favor when the merits are close.

The following describes: (1) how to approach writing a trial court brief; and (2) what components make up the trial court brief.

Approach and Preparation

Often an attorney will have little time to write a brief. Some briefs must be written in a matter of hours. Attorneys may have several weeks to write other briefs, like briefs in support of summary judgment motions. In either situation, your approach to writing the brief is important.

A. Set a Schedule

Writing a brief takes time. Once you know you have a brief to write, you should calendar the date your brief is due and create a to-do list. Provide yourself with mini-deadlines for researching, outlining, creating a first draft, revising, editing, and proofreading. This way you will ensure that you have a polished, finely-tuned brief ready to file on time.

B. Thoroughly Research

The basics, obvious though they may be, are worth repeating. When researching an unfamiliar legal issue, consider starting with secondary sources (e.g., treatises, legal encyclopedias, practice guides, hornbooks, law review articles), which will guide you to potentially relevant statutes and cases. Consult the annotated codes to find applicable cases. Once you have found relevant statutes and cases, carefully read them; do not rely on headnotes or digests. Update relevant cases using resources such as Shepard's or Keycite. After you have identified helpful authority for your position, evaluate the weight of those authorities and note where in your argument you will need them.

C. Outline

Once you have completed your initial research, you should outline the major points of your brief. By outlining, you force yourself to think through the logic of your position. Your outline is the roadmap you will follow in organizing and developing your first draft. The more detailed the outline, the more focused you will be in preparing the first draft. One way to begin an outline is to draft your Point Headings. Under each Point Heading, state the applicable rules you will be using and the rule's components. This will ultimately serve as your rule summary. You should also list the cases you intend to rely on. Briefly note why the case favors your position. If you will be making detailed comparisons of the case with your case, summarize the case's holding, facts, and the court's reasoning. You should also include in your outline contrary authority (authority you believe opposing counsel will rely upon), and a plan for rebutting your opponent's strongest arguments.

D. First, Second, and Third Drafts

Writers commonly treat their first draft as sacrosanct. Doing so is a mistake. If you have the time, prepare multiple drafts. If you do not have the time, make the time. After each draft, take time away from the draft before returning to the editing process. Use the checklists in this book to edit each draft methodically. Editing is not always a linear process. Generally, the rewriting process begins with big picture considerations and then delves into sentence-level and stylistic matters. With first drafts, you should focus on the substance and organization of the argument. As you work through your initial draft, you should expect to overhaul main arguments and organization. Resist, however, the temptation to tinker with wording and other small-scale matters. Fiddling around with the style only wastes time at this stage. You first need to make sure that you have the argument right.

> "*When you complete a first draft, you are too close to your writing to evaluate it objectively. Set the paper aside before you revise. In addition, allow time for several sets of revisions.*"
>
> —Jane N. Richmond, Legal Writing: Form & Function 233 (2002).

E. Edit Systematically

Once you are satisfied with the substance and organization of your argument, you should next examine your paragraph and sentence structure. Finally, proofread the draft: correct grammatical errors, eliminate typos, and check citation format. Use the checklists in this book. Do not begin at the start of the brief and edit through to the end in one sitting. You cannot possibly do everything at once, so work paragraph by paragraph, and systematically correct mistakes and improve your writing style. Carefully review each paragraph several times, focusing on the items listed in the checklists. Print the document and edit the hard copy. Reviewing a document on a computer screen may be fine when editing short paragraphs or sentences, but the cramped space of the computer screen makes getting a feel for and reviewing the structure of the whole document difficult. You will likely miss things if you edit solely on the computer screen.

F. Spell-Check and Find/Replace

Most word processing programs have spell-checkers and find-and-replace functions. Be certain to spell-check all documents before sending them to supervising attorneys, clients, or judges. Yet do not rely solely on spell-checkers. Spell-checkers will not flag correctly spelled words that are used incorrectly. Use the find-and-replace function to ensure that you catch typos the spell-checker can not identify (e.g., form → from, statue → statute, trail → trial, baring → barring).

> *"Spell Checker Poem:*
> *I have a spelling Checker; It cam with my PC.*
> *It clearly marks for my revue, Mistakes I cannot sea.*
> *I've run this poem threw it; I'm sure your pleased to no.*
> *Its letter perfect in it's weigh; My Checker tolled mi sew!*
> *Two rite with care is quite a feet, Of witch won should bee proud.*
> *And we mussed dew the best wee can, Sew flaws are knot aloud."*
>
> —Anonymous (quoted in Judge Gerald Lebovits, *Problem Words and Pairs in Legal Writing—Part IV*, 77 June N.Y. St. B.J. 64 (2005)).

G. Leave Ample Time to Proofread and Polish

Before sending the brief to your client or filing it with the court, you should proofread the brief carefully. Proofreading is a separate process from editing and always takes longer than you think. A few essentials in proofreading:

- Double-check that you have met all court requirements.
- Review every case used to ensure you have cited it correctly.
- Check every word of every sentence on every page before the brief leaves your desk.

One technique is to proofread a hard copy by placing a straight-edge ruler under each line as you read. This process forces you to focus on each line. Another technique is to read the brief aloud slowly, which forces you to focus more closely on each word. Finally, consider having a colleague read your work.

* * * * *

Trial Court Brief Fundamentals

Writing a persuasive trial court brief requires knowing what should be included in each section of the brief. Although formatting rules vary from court to court—and you must be certain to comply with local court rules—four basic components are common to trial court briefs: Introduction, Statement of Facts, Argument, and Conclusion.

A. Introduction

The Introduction, obviously, will be the first section read by the court. So start strong! Be certain that your Introduction includes a theme and states the upshot of your argument. Specifically, a good Introduction will: (1) briefly identify who the parties are, and what the case and the motion are about; (2) specifically request the precise relief sought (i.e., to grant or deny the motion); and (3) summarize the reasons why the court should rule in your favor.

In addition, an Introduction should advance a core theory of the argument that follows, should rarely refer to authority, and should rarely be longer than a page. *See* Appendix B for examples.

> "A 'winning brief' has to grab my attention at the earliest possible point, focusing me on the central nature of the case and the principal issues.... What is this dispute about? Why are you before the court?"
>
> —Hon. C. Kenneth Grosse, Washington Court of Appeals (quoted in Bryan A. Garner, *Judges on Briefing: A National Survey*, 8 SCRIBES J. LEGAL WRITING 1, 10 (2001–2002)).

B. Statement of Facts

Lawyers often underestimate the importance of the Statement of Facts: they choose to exclude it entirely or give it short shrift, or they include mind-numbing, irrelevant detail. Doing any of these things weakens the brief. The facts drive legal analysis. An effective Statement of Facts will be concise and shaded persuasively. It will include all facts mentioned in the brief's Argument section, and will never make arguments or state legal conclusions. The Statement should contain both procedural and substantive facts. Procedural facts include the parties' names, the claims and defenses, and the procedural posture surrounding the motion at issue. In contrast, substantive facts are facts germane to the issue. These are the facts the court will consider in deciding the motion. If your Statement of Facts is more than two or three pages long, consider using headings to divide the section.

Describe the facts in such a way that the court will be inclined to rule in your favor. After reading just the Statement of Facts, the judge should be thinking, "This side wins." To frame the facts persuasively, begin and end each paragraph with a favorable fact, or at the very least, a neutral fact. You have a duty to include facts unfavorable to your position, but you can neutralize them by placing them in the middle of paragraphs. Describe favorable facts in more detail than facts unfavorable to your position. Consider casting unfavorable facts abstractly or in the passive voice. You should describe favorable facts vividly, concretely, and in the active voice.

Here are a few "nevers" when writing a Statement of Facts: First, never exaggerate facts or dramatize them with hyperbole. Second, never omit critically pertinent facts, even those that work against your argument. Doing so will undermine your credibility (you can be sure opposing counsel will be bringing up those facts), risk raising the ire of the judge, and potentially lead to sanctions. Third, do not start every sentence with a date. Organizing facts chronologically is fine, but a list of dates is not a persuasive Statement of Facts. Finally, in general, do not quote the law or cite to it in the Statement of Facts.

C. Argument

An effective Argument section will: (1) begin with the strongest affirmative argument (unless, of course, you must address a threshold issue, such as jurisdiction); (2) be clearly organized with point headings and subheadings; (3) use thesis paragraphs, roadmaps, and signposts; and (4) address and refute the strongest of your opponent's arguments. Lawyers often overlook this last point. The best Arguments assert their own premises and conclusions *and* rebut arguments you anticipate in the Opposition brief.

> *"Be brief, be pointed; let your matter stand.*
> *Lucid in order, solid, and at hand;*
> *Spend not your words on trifles, but condense;*
> *Strike with the mass of thought, not drops of sense;*
> *Press to the close with vigor, once begun;*
> *And leave (how hard the task!) leave off, when done."*
>
> —Justice Joseph Story, *Advice To A Young Lawyer*,
> 5 Am. Jurist & L. Mag. 298 (1831).

D. Headings and Subheadings

An effective Argument section has commanding point headings. Your major point headings should be independent and complete, and provide free-standing grounds for a ruling in your favor. When listed in the Table of Contents, the headings and subheadings must lay out a complete, understandable, and persuasive outline of your position. Each heading should be: (1) an easily understandable, single sentence; and (2) a forceful and argumentative point. In major headings, as opposed to subheadings, the heading should identify the ruling sought. Each subheading should identify an independent reason that supports the ruling.

E. Conclusion

The Conclusion should be short and to the point. Do not summarize or restate your arguments. Instead, state the precise relief sought.

F. Table of Contents and Table of Authorities

Regardless of whether a court requires a Table of Contents or a Table of Authorities, excluding them is often a mistake. All briefs, except ones that are only a few pages long, should include these tables. In addition to making the brief look professional and complete, tables serve other, more important, purposes. First, they make life easier for judges. Judges often turn first to the tables to get an overview of the brief. A good Table of Contents will allow a judge to see, easily and quickly, the logic of your argument before turning to the brief's body. A Table of Authorities enables a judge to scan and assess the authorities you have relied on. Second, preparing the Table of Contents will require you to evaluate the structure of your analysis, and carefully consider whether your point headings could be phrased more effectively.

G. A Theory or Theme

In a trial brief, a good writer will convey a legal theme or theory that forms the brief's backbone. A good theory will intertwine both law and facts to explain why the court should rule in your client's favor. Frame your theory in a way that will minimize unfavorable facts and appeal to common sense, logic, and fairness. You should weave your theory of the case when making key points in the brief.

H. Types of Legal Argument

When writing your brief, keep in mind the various types of legal arguments you can make. These include: (1) arguments by definition (i.e., explaining why the elements of a rule are met, or not, by applying the element's definition to your case); (2) arguments by analogy (i.e., analogizing or distinguishing your case with the facts and reasoning of precedents); and (3) policy arguments (e.g., arguments discussing the positive or negative impact of the court's ruling on society, the development of the law, etc.). Lawyers regularly make arguments by definition, but all too often ignore the other argument types. In trial court briefs, policy arguments are generally less important than arguments based on precedent, because trial courts are in the business of applying the law rather than creating it. Nevertheless, even at the trial court level, policy arguments can be important in close cases, since the issue can turn on what outcome better supports the policy rationale of the applicable rule.

I. A Note on Tone

Avoid humor or excessive emotion in your writing. Trying to be humorous or groping at the judge's heartstrings is unprofessional, and judges and their clerks frown upon it. Be forthright and direct. Be a powerful advocate, but avoid injecting whimsy into your argument. Also, avoid melodrama. Never use over-the-top pleas to "apple pie" or the "American way."

* * * * *

Trial Court Brief Checklist

Use the following checklist after you are satisfied with the substantive arguments. Go through each step, systematically improving the brief.

Step 1: The Basics

First, review the brief to ensure that each component of the brief is complete.

A. Introduction

❑ Does the Introduction introduce the parties and briefly describe (1–2 sentences) the case?

❑ Does the Introduction identify the pending motion?

❑ Does the Introduction state the specific relief sought, and summarize why the court should rule in your favor?

B. Statement of Facts

❑ Does the Statement of Facts contain both procedural and substantive facts?

❑ Is the Statement of Facts concise, easy-to-follow, and, if necessary, separated in subsections by appropriate headings?

❑ Does the Statement of Facts contain all facts used in your Argument section?

❑ Is each fact in the Statement of Facts supported by an appropriate citation to declarations, pleadings, etc.?

❑ Does the Statement of Facts persuasively describe the facts?

❑ Does the Statement of Facts make an argument, or recite the law? If so, delete the argument or recitation of law.

C. Argument

- ❏ Does your Argument section contain clear and assertive point headings that echo and expand upon the points made in your Introduction?
- ❏ Does your Argument section have an easily understandable and accurate rule summary?
- ❏ Have you organized your Argument section around each component (e.g., element, factor) of the rule?
- ❏ Have you fully and accurately described precedents that merit comparison with your case?
- ❏ Have you effectively analogized or distinguished the precedent with your case?
- ❏ Have you considered the role, if any, of policy in advancing your argument?
- ❏ Does your Argument section refute or deflect your opponent's strongest arguments?
- ❏ Do you include roadmaps and signposts in your Argument section to make the structure of your argument easier to follow?
- ❏ Are your headings and subheadings argumentative and do they advance the argument?
- ❏ By reading only your headings and subheadings, is the organization of your Argument logical?

D. Conclusion

- ❏ Is your Conclusion short and to the point?
- ❏ Does it state the precise relief sought, in the same way as your Introduction?

* * * * *

Step 2: Now Use the Chapter 1 Checklists to Revise and Improve Your Writing Style

Chapter 3

Appellate Briefs

Most cases on appeal are won or lost on the brief. Judges (and their clerks) will often read and reread the briefs many times before rendering a decision. This chapter sets out the elements to writing strong and effective appellate briefs.

Approach and Preparation

An appellate brief in many ways is similar to a trial court brief. Of course, one difference between the two is that you usually have substantially less time to prepare a trial court brief. The longer lead time afforded in drafting the appellate brief permits writers more opportunity to organize and edit systematically. Below are some general guidelines for approaching and preparing to write an appellate brief.

A. Set a Schedule

As with trial court briefs, you should calendar the dates your brief is due and create a to-do list. Appellate briefs often are complicated, involve multiple issues, rely on a voluminous record, and require extended discussions of what the law is or ought to be. You must have enough time to complete the brief so that you can edit it carefully. You must also provide your client sufficient time to review and comment before filing.

B. Know the Record

To write a compelling appellate brief, mastering the record, both legally and factually, is essential. This includes carefully reviewing any testimony, documents, and exhibits submitted to the trial court. Only after becoming intimately familiar with the record will you be in a position to develop a theory of the case, and identify the specific issues upon which you intend to base your appeal. One way of becoming familiar with the record is through outlining or diagramming the major procedural and substantive events that occurred at the trial court level.

As you review the record, keep in mind what you must establish to have the court rule in your favor. If you represent the appellant, review the record with the following questions in mind: What trial court rulings are particularly vulnerable to attack? How significant were those rulings to the outcome of the case? Was the ruling based on the court's erroneous statement or application of the law, or was the ruling based on the court's factual findings? For the appellant, focusing on a few well-defined issues is critical. Be selective. In your appellate brief, you should not include every error the trial court made.

C. Thoroughly Research

An obvious point: at the outset of the brief-writing process, you must meticulously research the substantive law. Do not rely only on trial counsel's efforts; the appeal is a time to look at the case anew. When researching even familiar areas of law, consider starting with broad secondary sources (e.g., treatises, legal encyclopedias, practice guides, hornbooks, or law review articles), which will guide you to potentially relevant statutes and cases. Consult the annotated codes to find applicable cases. Once you have found relevant statutes and cases, carefully read them; do not rely on headnotes or digests. Update relevant cases using resources such as Shepard's or Keycite. After you have identified helpful authority for your position, evaluate the weight of those authorities and note where in your argument you will need them.

In many appeals, you may find it helpful or even necessary to expand your research universe beyond your jurisdiction, especially when arguments revolve around what the law ought to be. When weighing your authorities, keep in mind that cases outside your jurisdiction are persuasive only, and that cases from a state's highest court will carry more weight than cases from intermediate appellate courts. Secondary authorities, such as treatises and law review articles, while not binding authority, sometimes will contain valuable information supporting your position. All things being equal, however, prefer judicial opinions that support your position, rather than secondary sources.

D. Outline and Draft Point Headings

Once you have completed your initial research, you should outline your brief before writing. One way to do this is to first write your point headings and then structure your Argument around them. The reason for doing so is sound: by outlining you force yourself to think through the logic of your position. Failing to outline can result in missing key points, or drafting essential parts of the argument at the last minute.

Your outline is the roadmap that you will follow in organizing and developing your first draft. The more detailed the outline, the more focused you will be in preparing the first draft. For each issue on appeal, you should state the applicable rule of law and identify the rule's components. If the appeal requires that you establish each element of a rule, organize your outline element by element. Briefly define each element in your outline, and list favorable cases under each element. This process helps you put together your rule summary and gives you a preliminary way of organizing your argument. Briefly note why each precedent you will rely upon favors your position. If you will be making detailed comparisons of the precedent with your case, summarize the case's holding, facts, and the court's reasoning. You should also include in your outline contrary authority (authority that you believe opposing counsel will rely upon), and a plan for rebutting your opponent's strongest arguments.

E. Write Out Your Topic Sentences

In fleshing out the outline, consider drafting topic sentences for each section of the Appellate Brief. By first writing your topic sentences as logical conclusions, you force yourself to focus on what you must say in each paragraph. The paragraph thus becomes the building block upon which you create the brief.

F. First, Second, and Third Drafts

Follow the structure of your outline in preparing your first draft. Avoid writer's block by writing without restraint. Recognize the draft for what it is: a dump draft where you deposit all your thoughts in one place. Do not spend time trying to edit as you go along or thinking of ways to express an idea as artfully as possible. You will take care of those tasks in later drafts. If you are stymied on one part of the brief, move on to another part. You can then return to the problematic part with a fresher mind. As with trial court briefs, avoid treating your first draft of the appellate brief as sacrosanct. You will be relieved to have finished the draft and for good reason: the first draft of anything is generally the hardest one to produce. Your work, however, is far from done. Make time to go through multiple drafts. After each draft, you should provide yourself time away from the brief before further editing. Doing so will give you much-needed distance and allow you to revise more objectively. Use the checklists in this book to edit methodically.

"When it comes to writing for the public, you should fear more the danger of putting out slipshod work by omitting to revise it than that of delaying public business by excessive polishing. Very few can write what they mean and influence their readers precisely as they intend without revising their first attempt."

—Sir Ernest Gowers, The Complete Plain Words (Prologue)
(1948, rev. 1988).

G. Edit Systematically

When you are ready to begin editing, use the checklists provided in this book. For evaluating the overall organization of the brief, you should print the document and review the hard copy. Reviewing a document on a computer screen may be fine when editing short paragraphs or sentences, but the cramped space of the computer screen makes getting a feel for and reviewing the structure of the whole document difficult. You will likely miss mistakes if you edit solely on the computer screen. After you are satisfied with the large-scale organization, work paragraph by paragraph, systematically correcting mistakes and improving the writing style. Carefully review each paragraph several times, with each review focusing on the items listed in the checklists.

H. Spell-Check and Find/Replace

Most word processing programs have spell-checkers and find-and-replace functions. Be certain to spell-check all documents before sending them to supervising attorneys, clients, or judges. Yet do not rely solely on spell-checkers. Spell-checkers will not flag correctly spelled words that are used incorrectly. Use the find-and-replace function to ensure that you catch typos the spell-checker can not identify (e.g., form → from, statue → statute, trail → trial, baring → barring).

"When you look for typos, don't rely on a computer spell-checker. It is bound to miss things, particularly when you've used a word improperly rather than misspelled it. The Scribes Journal of Legal Writing used to collect such misprints and came up with a few doozies. There was a court filing addressed to the 'Horable U.S. District Judge.' And the brief signed, 'Rectfully submitted.'"

—Steven D. Stark, Writing to Win: The Legal Writer 51 (1999).

I. Leave Ample Time to Proofread and Polish

Before sending the brief to your client or filing it with the court, you should proofread the brief carefully. Proofreading is a separate process from editing and will always take longer than you think. A few essentials in proofreading:

- Double-check that you have met all court requirements.
- Review every case used to ensure you have cited it correctly.
- Check every word of every sentence on every page before the brief leaves your desk.

One technique is to proofread a hard copy by placing a straight-edge ruler under each line as you read. This process forces you to focus on each line. Another technique is to read the brief aloud slowly, which forces you to focus more closely on each word. Consider having a colleague read your work.

J. Follow the Rules

The court rules governing the form, content, and means of filing and serving an appellate brief vary from jurisdiction to jurisdiction. Judges and court clerks are serious about court rules and get annoyed when parties ignore them, or worse, attempt to circumvent them. Judges rarely excuse a lawyer's failure to comply with the rules. Before you finish writing your brief, ensure that you have scrupulously followed the applicable court rules.

* * * * *

Appellate Brief Fundamentals

Appellate brief requirements vary among the courts, and from the federal to state court systems. Certain sections, however, are common to almost all appellate briefs: Question Presented, Statement of the

Case, Standard of Review, Summary of Argument, Argument, and Conclusion. When writing each section, remember your goal is to persuade.

A. Question(s) Presented ("Statement of Issues")

The Question Presented orients the reader to the issue that the appellate court must decide. Most courts, therefore, require that the Question Presented section appear early in the brief. For each major issue on appeal, you should have a separate question presented.

A strong question presented will offer a crisp, well-defined legal question that frames the issue on appeal in your favor. Each question should: (1) be no more than a sentence long; (2) be crafted in such a way that it is answerable by a "yes"; and (3) identify the applicable rule followed by the most important facts favorable to your position. In other words, unless the issue on appeal is a pure question of law, do not write an abstract question presented. Instead, frame the issue by tying a legal principle to the key facts of the case. A common format for a question presented is "Under ... does ... when." In this format, the question asks "Under [the relevant law], does [a legal status or legal entitlement exist] when [certain legally significant facts are present].

A final point: courts often prefer that you refer to the parties in the question presented by descriptive terms (e.g., a nationwide beverage maker, a computer software company, a consumer, the property owner, the employee), and not by their names or legal titles. Legal titles (e.g., plaintiff, defendant, appellant, etc.) force the court to remember who the parties are in the case, making the Question Presented less readily understandable. *See, e.g.,* Fed. R. App. P. 28(d) (2006) (instructing attorneys not to use procedural titles in appellate briefs and at oral argument).

B. Statement of the Case

The Statement of the Case has two components: a summary of the case's procedural background, and a summary of the underlying, substantive facts. Together they describe the pertinent procedural history and the factual record relevant to the issues before the court. The procedural summary should identify the parties, the relevant claims or affirmative defenses, and the procedural route the case took to reach the appellate court.

As a general guideline, the Statement of the Case should: (1) be straightforward and easy to follow; (2) recount the relevant facts in an interesting and compelling way; and (3) advance a core theme favorable to your position. The Statement of the Case must accurately set forth the facts and be devoid of exaggeration and overstatement. Nevertheless, you should present the facts from your client's perspective and in a light advantageous to your client's position: emphasize favorable facts and downplay unfavorable facts. Insert subheadings at logical intervals. Your Statement of the Case should not go on for more than three or four pages without a heading.

A few other considerations to bear in mind. First, ensure that the opening paragraph starts strong. Avoid starting with a date (e.g., "In 2005….") or a chronological summary. Instead, the Statement of the Case should begin with a few sentences that set up the legal and procedural context. Second, the Statement of the Case should include every fact that you use in your Argument section. Third, support each fact with an accurate record cite. Never force a judge or her clerk to search through the record for an important fact. Lastly, you must not analyze the law, argue the issue, or draw factual inferences in the Statement of the Case—reserve these tactics for the Argument section.

C. Standard of Review

A common blunder of the inexperienced attorney is to ignore the Standard of Review. Do not do so. On appeal, the issue is not whether the appellant should have won below, but whether the trial court committed reversible error under the relevant standard of review. You must alert the appellate court to the applicable standard of review, and refer to the standard whenever necessary to buttress your arguments. Generally, three types of appellate review exist: (1) *de novo*; (2) abuse of discretion; and (3) clearly erroneous. *See* Fed. R. App. P. 28(a)(9)(B) (2006).

D. Summary of the Argument

A Summary of the Argument condenses your core arguments, while conveying the theory of your case. To do this effectively, you must state your main conclusion (e.g., why the lower court erred) and summarize why the application of the legal rules or principles to the critical facts supports that conclusion. The Summary should persuasively distill and logically preview the key parts of your Argument section. The Summary should never simply restate the Argument section's Point Headings. It should be short: only one or two pages long. One rule of thumb is to summarize your argument for each major issue in one paragraph.

"The summary of argument will likely create the first, and perhaps last, impression of the Court towards the legal merits of the client's case. It should be the structural centerpiece of the entire brief."

—David W. Burcham (quoted in Ruggero J. Aldisert, Winning on Appeal: Better Briefs and Oral Argument 184 (2d ed. 2003)).

E. The Argument

The Argument—complete with citations to the record and applicable legal authority—must address each issue on appeal. Each issue should have its own major heading and sub-headings, since each issue is an independent reason for the court to rule in your client's favor. In general, do not have more than two or three main headings. In most cases, a good Argument will advance only two or three reasons for reversal. If you represent appellee, you will have little choice but to respond to the issues raised by the appellant.

A few basics to remember: (1) order your points from strongest to weakest (unless, of course, you must first address threshold issues); (2) exclude frivolous arguments; (3) disclose and address relevant adverse authority; and (4) show how public policy supports your position. Public policy is especially important at the appellate level since judges often look beyond the facts of the case and want to know how their ruling may affect future cases involving similar issues. After making your arguments, refute and address the strongest of your opponent's arguments. Always weave in a consistent theme so that the judge has in mind your main point. Lastly, be selective in the points you make. Do not dilute your best arguments with weak ones.

"Strike for the jugular, let go of the rest."

—Justice Oliver Wendell Holmes
(quoted in MARIA L. CIAMPI & WILLIAM H. MANZ,
THE QUESTION PRESENTED: MODEL APPELLATE BRIEFS 2 (2000)).

F. Point Headings

As with the Trial Court brief, an effective Argument section will contain forceful headings and subheadings (known collectively as point headings). Each major heading should be an independent and complete reason for the court to rule in your client's favor. Each point heading should be readily understandable and one sentence long (not two or more sentences long and not a phrase). Point headings break up long arguments into easy-to-digest segments. You should avoid having more than three pages of text without a heading or subheading.

Effective major headings will often set forth: (1) an action you want the court to take (e.g., reverse the trial court) or a conclusion the court should draw (e.g., the trial court erred); and (2) the reasons why the court should take the action or reach the conclusion. Subheadings to the major heading should then be independent reasons that support the assertion set forth in the major heading. An example of a major heading: "The trial court erred when it [set forth ruling] … because [set forth reason why the court erred].…"

G. Conclusion

The Conclusion should be no longer than a sentence or two. It should state the precise relief you seek, and identify, in simple terms, the grounds on which the court should base its relief. The judge should know immediately what relief you want from skimming the Conclusion section. Example: "For the foregoing reasons, this Court should reverse the District Court's judgment and remand the case for a new trial."

H. Table of Contents and Authorities

A precise and accurate Table of Contents is essential to all appellate briefs, and is normally required by court rules. The Table of Contents is the first section a judge will most likely read, and a judge will continually refer back to the Table of Contents when reviewing the case. Like the Summary of the Argument, the Table of Contents provides a judge with a quick overview of your argument and discloses the argument's logic.

A Table of Authorities is equally important because it enables a judge to scan the statutes, precedents, and secondary authorities you have relied on. You should include in your Table of Authorities every authority you cite to in your brief, and a reference to every page in the brief on which that authority appears. As a general rule, categorize your Table of Authorities by cases, then constitutional and statutory authority, and finally secondary authorities. In each category, you should list the authorities in alphabetical order (generally, cases in alphabetical order by first named party, statutes in order of their title and section number in ascending order, secondary sources by the author's last name or if appropriate by the title of the source). Make sure that each authority is full-cited properly. Do not include pinpoint cites in your table.

* * * * *

> *"Regardless of the panel you get, the questions you get or the answers you give, I maintain it is the brief that does the final job, if for no other reason than that opinions are often written several weeks and sometimes months after the argument. The arguments, great as they may have been, are forgotten. In the seclusion of his chambers the judge has only his briefs and the law books. At that time your brief is your only spokesman."*
>
> —Justice Thurgood Marshall (quoted in Carole C. Berry, Effective Appellate Advocacy: Brief Writing and Oral Argument 66 (3d ed. 2003)).

Appellate Brief: Other Considerations

A. The Tone

As with all brief writing, your tone and writing style must be professional and forceful, without being arrogant or ostentatious. Avoid inflammatory language, flippancy, colloquialisms, or melodramatics. Omit humor. Never attempt to impress the appellate court by using unnecessary foreign words, archaisms, or legal jargon.

> *"Your tone should be calm, forthright, and unflinching. It should not be heated, accusatory, defensive, or hyperbolic. You'll persuade by forcefully stating—but never overstating—the legal and factual support for your position. Ideally, you should set all this out in an interesting, engaging way."*
>
> —Bryan A. Garner, The Redbook: A Manual on Legal Style 403 (2d ed. 2006).

B. A Theory or Theme

The best appellate briefs advance a core theory of the case to unify the argument. You should ground the theory (or theme) in the record, the law, sound public policy, and basic notions of fairness. Frame your theory of the case in a way that will explain away unfavorable facts and appeal to common sense, logic, and fairness. You should weave in your theory of the case when making key points in the brief.

C. Roadmaps, Signposts, and Thesis Paragraphs

Consider including, between your major point headings and subheadings, a roadmap of the points made in the next subsections. Do not needlessly repeat what your argument is, but orient the reader as to what is to come. Doing so will increase the persuasiveness and readability of your appellate brief, by giving the court the big picture of your argument.

D. Using Authority in Appellate Briefs

In addition to the suggestions in Chapter 1 about using authority, here are a few other suggestions you should consider for your appellate brief. First, many attorneys resort to "cute" quotations from literature or popular culture. Rarely, if ever, are these sorts of quotations effective. Second, when relying on precedents, keep in mind whether they are controlling or merely persuasive. Appellate courts initially are concerned with the law of their jurisdiction, but they also are concerned about how their ruling will affect future cases. When assessing the weight of authority, ask yourself: Is the law settled or one of first impression? Is the law ripe for revisiting and modifying or even eliminating? What approaches have other jurisdictions adopted?

E. Types of Legal Argument

When writing your brief, keep in mind the various types of legal arguments you can make. These include: (1) arguments by definition (i.e., explaining why the elements of a rule are met, or not, by applying the element's definition to your case); (2) arguments by analogy (i.e., analogizing or distinguishing your case with the facts and reasoning of precedents); and (3) policy arguments (e.g., arguments discussing the positive or negative impact of the court's ruling on society, the development of the law, etc.). Lawyers regularly make arguments by definition, but all too often ignore other argument types. Policy arguments are important when the court is interpreting the rule and of course when the existence of the rule itself is at issue. Policy arguments are especially important in appellate briefs, since the issues often turn on what outcome better supports the policy rationale of the applicable rule.

> "Although judges and practitioners may disagree about the relative importance of oral argument in the appellate process, no one disagrees with the fundamental proposition that the brief is by far and away the most important feature of the appeal.... [M]ost cases are won or lost on the briefs."
>
> —William J. Bauer & William C. Bryson, *The Appeal*, THE DOCKET 12 (1987) (quoted in BRADLEY G. CLARY ET AL., ADVOCACY ON APPEAL 30 (2d ed. 2004)).

F. The Reply Brief

Here are some suggestions regarding reply briefs. First, you should always file a reply brief, if permitted. This is your last opportunity to persuade the court in writing. Second, never merely rehash arguments made in your opening brief. An effective reply brief should respond to and rebut the specific arguments raised in the opposing brief. When rebutting the other side's argument, frame your topic sentences assertively rather than defensively. Your topic sentence should not just merely reiterate the other side's argument. Instead, frame the topic sentences as assertive premises favoring your position. Third, if your opponent misstates the record, authority, or your arguments, focus the court's attention on those misstatements and correct them. Fourth, a reply brief should be no longer than necessary to defuse the other side's strong points. Effective reply briefs are concise, focused, and to the point.

* * * * *

Appellate Brief Checklist

Use the following checklist after you have written several drafts of the appellate brief and are satisfied with the substantive arguments. Go through each step, systematically improving the brief.

Step 1: The Basics

First, review the brief to ensure that each component of the brief is complete.

A. Question(s) Presented

❑ Does the Question Presented section focus on one or two well-defined issues that are at the heart of the appeal?

❑ Is each Question Presented a single sentence long?

❑ Is each Question Presented answerable with a "yes"?

❑ Does the Question Presented identify the rule applicable to the issue and the most important facts favorable to your position?

❑ Have you used descriptive terms to refer to the parties, rather than their names or legal titles?

B. Statement of the Case

❑ Does the Statement of the Case summarize both the procedural background of the case and the underlying substantive facts relevant to the issues?

❑ Does your Statement of the Case: (1) contain all facts used in your Argument section; and (2) recite only facts, rather than make arguments or cite to the law?

❑ Is every sentence of your Statement of the Case supported with accurate citations to the record?

❑ Is the Statement of the Case simple and easy to follow, and does it tell a compelling story favorable to your client?

❑ Does the Statement of the Case advance a core theme or theory of the case on appeal?

❑ If the Statement of the Case is several pages long, have you used headings and, possibly, subheadings?

C. Standard of Review and Summary of Argument

❑ Does your appellate brief have a short, easy-to-understand Standard of Review section that sets forth the standard of review for each major issue?

❑ Do you refer to the Standard of Review when appropriate in the Argument section to buttress your arguments?

❑ Does your Summary of the Argument section advance a core theme/theory of the case?

❑ Does your Summary of Argument distill and preview the key components of the Argument section?

❑ Is your Summary of Argument section short: generally one paragraph for each major issue?

D. Argument

❑ Does your Argument section contain clear point headings that echo the points made in your Summary of the Argument?

❑ Does each Point Heading state an independent reason for the court to rule in your favor?

❑ Are your Point Headings argumentative and do they advance the argument?

❑ Based only upon your Point Headings, is the organization of your Argument clear and logical?

❑ Does your Argument section begin with your strongest argument? If not, have you first addressed threshold issues?

❑ Does your Argument show how policy supports your position?

❑ Does your Argument section address adverse authority?

❑ Does your Argument section address your opponent's strongest arguments or authority, and refute or deflect them?

❏ Do you include roadmaps or signposts in your Argument section to make the structure of your argument easier to follow?

❏ Is your theme/theory of the case weaved in throughout your Argument section?

E. *Conclusion and Tables*

❏ Is your Conclusion short and to the point?

❏ Does your Conclusion state the precise relief sought?

❏ Do you have a Table of Contents? Is each page number cited to accurately?

❏ Have you avoided using bold, underline, or italics in the Table of Contents?

❏ Do you have a Table of Authorities? Have you properly cited each authority, based on the applicable citation guide?

❏ Is the formatting of the Table of Contents and Table of Authorities professional looking?

* * * * *

Step 2: Now Use the Chapter 1 Checklists to Revise and Improve Your Writing Style

Chapter 4

Effective Oral Argument

Whether before a state or federal trial court, an appellate court, or the United States Supreme Court, oral advocacy can play a significant role in how judges decide cases. Once the parties have filed their briefs, oral argument is the only chance for the parties to stand face to face with the court and argue their case. Done well, oral advocacy helps the court in its deliberative process. The effective advocate directly addresses the judges' questions and concerns, and places the judges at ease with the advocate's position. Unfortunately, many advocates—even skilled attorneys—forget the basics, and the oral presentation becomes long-winded, rambling, and ultimately unhelpful. The following, we hope, will remind attorneys and students of the fundamentals of effective oral advocacy.

Approach and Preparation

The effectiveness of an oral argument depends almost entirely on your level of preparation. No substitutes exist for the hard work needed to know the record, the law, the arguments, and the answers to the difficult questions that the court will undoubtedly ask you.

A. Create a Schedule

To ensure that you have time to properly prepare, create a comprehensive to-do list at the start of the preparation process and then stick to it. Be careful; it is easy to underestimate the time necessary to prepare.

> "[T]here are three secrets for arguing well in the Supreme Court: preparation, preparation, and still more preparation."
>
> —General William K. Suter (quoted in David C. Frederick, The Art of Oral Advocacy 13 (2003)).

B. Develop a Theme

Never underestimate the importance of a theme: an overarching principle that ties together the various parts of your argument. The theme can center on a straightforward application of undisputed law to fact. Or a theme can focus on the fairness of a particular outcome. Or a theme can be developed around important public policies. A theme is especially useful in factually or legally complex cases. When the questioning during an oral argument gets tough, you can return to your theme and reinforce the central aspects of your argument. Early on in your preparation, you should struggle with reducing the issues in the case to a short statement that reveals "what this case is about."

C. Know the Record

A good attorney has no excuse for failing to know the record cold. You are bound to get questions from the bench about the record, and you cannot afford to be unprepared. If chronology is important to the argument, put together a timeline of key events and include record citations next to each event. Inexperienced and hastily prepared attorneys often do not know the record well enough — a common criticism the bench has of the appellate bar.

D. Master the Authority

At the oral argument, you must know the relevant law, including: (1) pertinent provisions and key language of statutes; and (2) the holdings, facts, and reasoning of key cases, especially cases decided by the court before which you are to appear. Be certain to update your authority just before the argument so that you are armed with the latest legal developments.

E. The Standard of Review

Make certain you understand what the standard of review is, and how the standard of review applies to your argument. You are almost certain to get questions about the Standard of Review.

F. Prepare an Organized Set of Notes

When you approach the podium, you should take with you a set of organized, easily accessible notes in a professional looking folder or binder. Your notes should include the following: (1) a list of essential facts (both procedural and substantive) with record citations; (2) a list of key authorities; and (3) a bullet-point outline of the essential aspects of your argument, with your arguments ordered in descending importance. Keep your notes to a minimum, since you should not waste time (and risk flustering yourself) by flipping through pages of material. For that reason, taking your brief up to the lectern is a bad idea. In addition, format your notes in a font size that you can easily read when placed at the lectern, without you having to bend down. Do not take with you a prepared written speech. You will have little or no opportunity to make extended canned comments. In addition, reading at the podium is a definite no-no, since it takes away from the immediacy of the arguments and places distance between you and the judges.

G. Do Moot Court

If the three keys to purchasing real estate is location, location, location, the three keys to an effective oral argument is practice, practice, practice. To prepare for an appellate oral argument, good attorneys recognize the importance of mooting. Have colleagues serve as moot court judges, and consider video-taping or audio-taping the practice rounds. When preparing: (1) spend time with your colleagues talking about the case, so that they are familiar with the key issues (an initial chat will greatly facilitate their understanding of the briefs); (2) provide your moot judges copies of the briefs; (3) prepare a list of sample questions that probe the weaker parts of your argument; and (4) ask colleagues, as part of their preparation, to come up with hypotheticals for you to address during the moot court round. After the practice argument, have your colleagues provide feedback, both positive and negative. If done properly, a moot court may take an hour or two.

H. Prepare Questions/Answers

Create a file of all possible questions that you think the court may ask you. Consider using note cards. On the front, write the question. On the back, write the answer. Creating and then reviewing the questions and answers will help you prepare properly.

I. Know Your Panel

Research the background of the judges you will be appearing before. Ask members of your firm and colleagues if they have had any recent experience with the panel assigned to the case. Before the oral argument, you should have a sense of each judge's legal philosophy and temperament. Knowing this information may help you choose which arguments to emphasize.

* * * * *

> *"You must prepare. You must know and—what is important—you must believe that you know, more about the case than anyone else in the courtroom, including the judges."*
>
> —Ruggero J. Aldisert, Winning on Appeal: Better Briefs and Oral Argument 310 (2d ed. 2003).

Oral Argument Fundamentals

A. The Opening

A good oral advocate will have memorized the opening of the argument. For most courts, attorneys should begin with "May it please the Court…." An effective opening includes: (1) an introduction of counsel and client; (2) a brief statement of the main issue on appeal, which also places the case in procedural context; and (3) a request to reserve time for rebuttal, if you are allowed rebuttal. After this opening, the advocate should signpost for the court the two or three main points the advocate intends to make. The signposts should be succinct, easily followed, and advance your theme or theory of the case. Remember, the first few sentences out of your mouth—that show confidence and professionalism—will set the tone for the argument.

B. Argument

In many oral arguments, responding to the justices' questions will take up most of your time. If you have the opportunity to make a freestanding argument, be certain to: (1) develop your arguments logically; (2) support your arguments with authority; and (3) be prepared to elaborate on each argument, discussing the law, the facts, and the policy. If multiple issues are on appeal, clearly indicate which issue you are discussing and avoid jumping back and forth among the issues.

C. Conclusion

You want to end on a strong note. To do this, avoid lengthy conclusions or recaps. The conclusion should be tight and to the point, and indicate precisely the relief you seek. If your time is running out (e.g., with one minute or less remaining), avoid raising a completely new argument. Instead, state your conclusion, thank the court, and then sit down. Generally, you should end before your time expires. If your time has expired (i.e., the red light is on), you must immediately stop speaking and ask for permission before proceeding. If the court grants permission, be very brief in finishing your point, thank the court, and then sit down.

D. Rebuttal

Rebuttal may be the hardest part of the oral argument. Without being pre-scripted, the rebuttal's purpose is to refute key points the opposing counsel has made. Do not make additional points, elaborate on key issues from your opening, summarize your arguments, or waste time nitpicking on irrelevant or side issues. Advocates rarely have much time for rebuttal, so your rebuttal should be focused and to-the-point. A good rebuttal will address one or possibly two points, but no more. It will be clear, forceful, and easy to understand. The shortest rebuttals are often the best.

* * * * *

Forensics and Presentation

A. Eye Contact

You should make eye contact with every member of the panel and do so naturally. When asked a question, do not focus solely on the questioner; scan the entire bench while answering. You want to ensure that no judge feels left out of the discussion.

B. Presentation/Speaking Style

Avoid reading your notes. An oral argument is not the time to read your brief or give a speech. Oral argument is a formal conversation, a dialogue to convince the court of your position's merits. Be certain to: (1) speak in a natural, conversational tone—avoid speaking in a monotone or too fast; (2) speak in short, easily understandable sentences; and (3) use inflection to emphasize important points. Throughout your argument, you should be professional and respectful. Inexperienced advocates often make the mistake of speaking too rapidly, or with too much passion and rhetoric.

C. Gestures

Keep gestures to a minimum. Wild arm-waving will not persuade a panel; even nervous gestures can be distracting. Control your hands. You may use your hands to emphasize a key point, but do not distract the court by overdoing it. Make certain that your gestures appear natural and comfortable. Of course, do not forget the basics: stand up straight, speak clearly, and never point at the justices.

D. Professionalism

Your credibility is everything. You must never: (1) insult opposing counsel; (2) use sarcasm; or (3) show anger, frustration, or temper with the court. Remember a judicial proceeding—whether trial or appellate—is a formal setting.

E. Be Respectful, Not Obsequious

You must accord the Court respect. When disagreeing with the Court, saying "Respectfully, no your honor...." may be appropriate. Inexperienced advocates, however, will often overdo it. Peppering your presentation with excessive *respectfullys* and *your honors* sounds hollow and obsequious.

> *"Always avoid words and phrases that distance you from your client or your client's position. Examples, which you may hear even from seasoned advocates, include: 'it is my client's position ...' or 'it is our contention that ...' or 'we believe...' Not only are such phrases inartful and wasteful of the precious minutes you are allotted, they have the effect of making it appear as if you may not really be standing behind your client's position—that you merely are paying lip-service to arguments your client has instructed you to make ."*
>
> —BRADLEY G. CLARY ET AL.,
> ADVOCACY ON APPEAL 123 (2d ed. 2004).

F. Personal Pronouns

Personal pronouns (*I, we, us*) generally should not be used in oral argument. Do not say, "We argue that the lower court erred...." Instead say, "Appellant argues that the lower court erred...." Better yet, simply make the point without ascribing the position to your client at all (e.g., "The trial court erred....").

* * * * *

Answering Questions

Answering questions from the bench is the most important aspect of oral argument. Questions give you a glimpse into what the judges think about the case, but they also give you an opportunity to persuade the court that your position is the correct one. Your answers to questions permit you to clarify or emphasize points made in the brief.

A. Be Composed

When a judge asks a question, the likely purpose is to obtain information, to seek clarification on troubling aspects of the case, or to make a point to other judges who may be on the fence or who may disagree with your position. If you do not know the answer to a question, never fake an answer. Never argue with the bench, and never appear irritated. When the other side presents its argument, be attentive and maintain a stoic façade.

> "*You must never show annoyance or frustration over being interrupted by a question. Do not ever snort or roll your eyes or fume when you are repeatedly interrupted. It is much more important to answer all the panel's questions than it is to get through your outline.*"
>
> —Michael D. Murray & Christy H. DeSanctis,
> Appellate Advocacy and Moot Court 169 (2006).

B. Never Interrupt or "Step on the Bench"

Few things can undermine an attorney's argument more than interrupting a judge. When a judge begins speaking, the attorney must stop immediately, even if the attorney is in the middle of a point or a sentence. As soon as a judge speaks, immediately stop speaking, listen to what is being asked, and after the judge is finished (do not overeagerly interrupt) respond with the best possible answer. Collect your thoughts and pause a moment before responding.

C. Answer Directly

You must directly answer the court's questions. A few nevers: (1) never tell the court that you will get to the question later; (2) never give even the slightest appearance of being evasive or exasperated; and (3) never ask questions of the court, except to clarify the question's meaning. If the question calls for a *yes* or *no*, respond with a *yes* or *no* and then explain your answer. When appropriate, provide what is known as a "heading response"—a short, pithy answer that will often signpost your answer (e.g., "Yes, for two reasons...." "No, that is not accurate. Let me explain...."). Lastly, do not ramble. If you feel you have answered the question, move on to your next point. Do not pause too long. If the court wants to follow-up, it will interject another question.

D. Concede Skillfully

A common error of the inexperienced advocate is to fear conceding any point. Being unnecessarily stubborn will only damage your argument and credibility, and waste precious time. Carefully consider what you can concede and what you cannot. If the point is trivial, concede it, and explain why the point is immaterial. Then move on.

E. Address Adverse Authority

Be prepared to address adverse authority; do not ignore it. Either argue that: (1) the authority does not apply to the issue before the court or is distinguishable from your case; or (2) the case was wrongly decided and provide cogent reasons why.

F. Hit Softballs out of the Park

Sometimes judges will ask questions favorable to your position (perhaps as a veiled message to the other judges). If a question appears sympathetic to your position, do not be suspicious of it. Answer the question by emphasizing the point's importance to your argument and reaffirm the correctness of your position.

G. Transition Skillfully

The best oral advocates use questions—even questions skeptical of the advocate's position—as an opportunity to transition the court back to affirmative points that persuade the court of the position's soundness. Although you must defer to the court and directly answer the questions posed, you should constantly attempt to assert control over the argument by leading the court to the points you wish to emphasize. Before the day of argument, you should practice transitioning (also known as segueing), and think through likely questions that will provide an opportunity to transition to strong positions.

* * * * *

Oral Argument Checklist

Use the following checklist to prepare for the Oral Argument.

Step 1: Preparation

Have you done the necessary preparation to ensure a strong oral argument? Ask yourself the following:

❑ Have you developed a theme or theory of the case? Can you explain to colleagues what your case is about in a few short sentences?

❑ Do you know the record cold?

❑ Are you well-versed on the authorities you rely on, and the authorities that your opponent relies on?

❑ Are you clear what the standard of review is for each issue on appeal?

❑ Have you prepared a list of likely questions? Can you answer them?

❑ Have you researched your panel? Have you asked firm members and colleagues for information about the judges? Do you know the predilections, temperament, and pet peeves of the judges who will be hearing the argument?

❑ Have you mooted? Have you videotaped or audiotaped the practice rounds? Have you reviewed these tapes objectively?

❑ Have you prepared an oral argument binder/set of notes that contain key information and a bullet-point outline of the essentials to your argument?

Step 2: The Components of the Oral Argument

Once you have done the necessary preparation, assess how well you have prepared the key components of the oral argument.

❑ Have you memorized an effective opening to the argument?

❑ Does the opening start with "May it please the Court"?

❑ Does your opening introduce yourself and your client, briefly state the issues on appeal, reserve time for rebuttal (if you represent appellant), and signpost the two or three main points you intend to make?

❑ Have you thought through hand gestures?

❑ Do you know your argument well enough that throughout the argument you can maintain eye contact with the panel?

❑ Have you practiced pacing and presentation style to ensure an easily understood argument?

❑ Have you refrained from using personal pronouns in your argument?

❑ Have you practiced answering the expected difficult questions? Do you know the answers?

❑ Have you thought through direct answers to key questions that provide yes, no, or heading responses?

❑ Have you carefully considered what points you can concede without damaging your argument?

❑ Are you prepared to address adverse authority? Can you explain why the authority does not apply, or why it is distinguishable?

❑ Have you worked out transitions and segues to lead the court back to the points you wish to emphasize?

❑ Have you thought about and practiced a short conclusion that permits you to end on a strong note?

❑ Have you practiced doing a short, focused rebuttal that refutes no more than one or two key points that opposing counsel made?

Step 3: The Day of the Oral Argument

Lastly, the night before or on the day of the oral argument:

❑ Reread your briefs and the other parties' briefs.

❑ Update the law.

❏ Review key portions of the record that you intend to rely on in your argument, or that you expect opposing counsel to rely on.

❏ Confirm that you have your oral argument binder/notes in your briefcase.

❏ Bring with you copies of key cases, or key documents from the record.

❏ Leave yourself plenty of time to arrive at the courthouse early.

❏ An obvious one: but are you in the appropriate business attire?

Chapter 5

Interoffice Memorandum

Before advocacy comes understanding. An Interoffice Memorandum is a written explanation, based on research, of the writer's analysis regarding a legal issue. The memorandum's purpose usually is to analyze and evaluate—in an objective, dispassionate, and thorough way—a legal problem for a more senior attorney or other decision-maker, who then decides how to proceed. For the senior attorney to choose the best course of action, the interoffice memorandum must demonstrate mastery of the applicable law and objectively ascertain and analyze the strengths and weaknesses of the client's position. Several attorneys will likely read an office memorandum many times; a well-written memorandum will remain a valuable resource long after it has served its immediate purpose. Here are some guidelines for writing effective memoranda.

Approach and Preparation

Frequently, a supervising or senior attorney will assign junior attorneys or clerks the task of drafting the interoffice memorandum. Also, judicial law clerks and externs prepare memoranda for judges to evaluate motions pending before the court. Student research assistants prepare memoranda for their professors. And as attorneys know quite well, the memorandum is a rite of passage for first-year law students. Drafting the memorandum requires competency in several essential skills: following instructions, managing facts, understanding and analyzing legal issues, performing research, organizing analysis, and, of course, writing clearly.

While the memorandum will inform the reader of the writer's analysis of the legal issue presented, the memorandum may serve other, less obvious, purposes as well. Many first-year students looking for summer employment will often use the memoranda that they wrote in their legal writing course as a writing sample. Lawyers frequently ask their law clerks or summer associates to prepare memoranda. The quality of the student's memoranda is an important factor when lawyers decide whether to extend an offer to the student. A sunny disposition will seldom overcome poorly prepared written work.

A. Be Certain You Understand the Task

The most thoroughly researched, insightful, and beautifully written memorandum will be useless if it fails to address what the supervisor wanted. Because attorneys are busy, sometimes even frenzied, they often make vague requests about the assignment. Make sure you are clear about the assignment. If you are at all unsure, ask specific questions. Most importantly, you must know precisely the issue you are to address. You should also know the memorandum's purpose (e.g., to assess the viability of making a particular motion, to determine the probability of success at trial, to advise the client about the pros and cons of a possible transaction). Because legal analysis depends on facts and law, you need to know what facts you are to assess. Are you supposed to gather the facts? Where can they be found? What is the law you are supposed to research and apply? You should also meet your supervisor's administrative requirements. When is the deadline? Who should be copied? Is there a recommended page limit?

As you work on the memorandum, you may have questions about the assignment. Ask the supervisor, if you can. If not, ask a colleague familiar with the case. Make sure, in other words, that you are on the right track. A tip: before you begin writing, check whether the firm has any previous work on the topic you are addressing.

B. Set a Schedule

With your memorandum's due date firmly in mind, you should figure out how you will manage your time to meet the deadline. Spending two weeks researching the issue, and one day reading your research and drafting the memorandum, is hardly a recipe for success. Divide your time into manageable tasks. If you have to gather facts from a boxful of files, allocate time for that. Allocate sufficient time for researching and reading your research. Leave ample time for drafting and, importantly, for revising and editing your work. If possible, finish your draft well before the deadline so that you can show your draft to the supervising attorney.

C. Thoroughly Research

If you are unfamiliar with a particular area of law, consult treatises, legal encyclopedias, practice guides, hornbooks, or law review articles. If your issue is statutory, check the annotated codes. Once you have found potentially relevant statutes and cases, read them carefully; do not rely on headnotes or digests. If your research becomes voluminous, organize your research by grouping your sources coherently (e.g., by rule, by element, by jurisdiction). Update relevant cases using resources such as Shepard's or Keycite.

D. Outline Your Memo

As is true for brief writing, your outline of the memorandum is the roadmap that you will follow in organizing and developing your first draft. The more detailed the outline, the more focused you will be in preparing the first draft. Start putting together the draft. Write out those sections you feel secure about. That would include, of course, your issue statements, since you will be certain about your assignment. Draft your facts, perhaps by first using bullet points for all the important facts. By now, you will have command over the general rules governing the issue. Draft your rule summary by identifying the statutes or cases that set forth the applicable rules. If you have cases that you will compare to the facts underlying your issue, summarize those cases. If you will be analyzing two or more elements or factors of the rule, put a sub-heading for each element or factor in your Discussion section.

One approach is to state the applicable rule of law and identify the rule's components for each issue. If the issue requires that you establish each element of a rule, organize your outline element by element. Provide a brief definition for each element, and list favorable cases under each element. Briefly indicate why that case favors your position. You should also include in your outline contrary authority (authority you believe opposing counsel will rely upon), and a plan for rebutting your opponent's strongest arguments.

E. Write Out Your Topic Sentences

In fleshing out the outline, write out your topic sentences for each section of the memorandum. By first writing your topic sentences as conclusions, you force yourself to focus on what you intend to say in each paragraph. The paragraph thus becomes the building block upon which the memorandum is created.

F. First, Second, and Third Drafts

Follow the structure of your outline to prepare your first draft. Avoid writer's block by writing without restraint. Recognize the draft for what it is: a dump site where you deposit all your thoughts in one place. Do not spend needless time editing as you go along or thinking of ways to express an idea as artfully as possible. Those are tasks that you take care of in later drafts. If you are stymied on one part of the brief, move on to another part. You can then return to the problematic part with a fresher mind. Avoid treating your first draft as sacrosanct. Make time to go through multiple drafts.

G. Edit Systematically

When you are ready to begin editing, use the checklists provided in this book. First, assess the memorandum's organization. For evaluating the overall organization of the memorandum, you should print the document and review the hard copy. You will likely miss things if you edit solely on the computer screen. Reviewing a document on a computer screen may be fine when editing short paragraphs or sentences, but the cramped space of the computer screen makes getting a feel for and reviewing the structure of the whole document difficult. After you are satisfied with the organization, work paragraph by paragraph, systematically correcting mistakes and improving writing style. Carefully review each paragraph several times, with each review focusing on the items in the checklists.

H. Spell-Check and Find/Replace

Most word processing programs have spell-checkers and find-and-replace functions. Be certain to spell-check all documents before sending them to supervising attorneys, clients, or judges. Yet do not rely solely on spell-checkers. Spell-checkers will not flag correctly spelled words that are used incorrectly. Use the find-and-replace function to ensure that you catch common typos the spell-checker can not identify (e.g., form → from, statue → statute, trail → trial, baring → barring).

I. Leave Ample Time to Proofread and Polish

Before sending the memorandum to your supervisor, you should proofread it carefully. Proofreading is a process separate from editing and will take longer than you think. A few essentials in proofreading:

- Double-check that you have met your supervisor's format requirements.

- Check every word of every sentence on every page before the memorandum leaves your desk.
- Review every case used to ensure you have cited it correctly.

One technique is to proofread a hard copy by placing a straight-edge ruler under each line as you read. Doing so forces you to focus on each line. Another technique is to read the memorandum aloud slowly, which forces you to focus on each word.

Memorandum Components

Formats vary from law firm to law firm, and even from lawyer to lawyer, but memoranda are usually divided into six sections: (1) the Heading; (2) Issue Statement; (3) Brief Answer; (4) Statement of Facts; (5) Discussion; and (6) Conclusion. Each section is discussed below.

A. The Heading

The precise formatting varies with the supervisor, but a memorandum heading should identify: (1) the intended recipient; (2) the writer; (3) the date on which the memorandum was completed; and (4) the subject, i.e., a "Re:" line stating the topic and, if appropriate, the client's identifying number. Usually a memorandum will begin with the word "MEMORANDUM" centered at the top of the page. The heading section is often divided from the memorandum body with a single line across the page. If your firm or office has a template, follow it.

B. Issue Statement ("Question Presented")

As the lead off to the memorandum, the Issue Statement—sometimes referred to as the Question Presented—should state the question or questions that the memorandum addresses. Issue Statements are commonly phrased as a question about whether a legal rule is satisfied, or how a court will likely rule in a particular dispute. Because your analysis in the memorandum will be objective, you should write your Issue Statements so that they are objective and do not state legal conclusions. The Issue Statement, therefore, should include the most favorable fact or facts for each party on that issue. A poor Issue Statement often is one devoid of necessary facts (e.g., "Did the defendant breach the contract?"). Better Issue Statements first identify the rule and then the key facts. Sometimes, however, the memorandum addresses only abstract legal principles, making facts unnecessary in the Issue Statement (e.g., "When are punitive damages available in a breach of contract action?"). An Issue Statement should be concisely written and easily understood, and is typically a single sentence. If there is more than one Issue Statement, each one should be a separate paragraph and the Issue Statements should be in the order in which they are analyzed in the Discussion section.

Several formats for writing Issue Statements exists. A common format is "Under ... does ... when." In this format, the question asks "Under [the relevant law], does [a legal status or legal entitlement exist] when [certain legally significant facts are present]." Another, less conventional, format is to write a short introduction. Under this approach, the Issue Statement is written by writing two or three short sentences detailing the crucial facts, and then a short sentence posing the legal question.

C. Brief Answer

The Brief Answer—sometimes referred to as the Summary Answer or the Short Conclusion—should directly follow the Issue Statement(s). The Brief Answer should answer the Issue Statement and concisely explain why the writer has reached that answer. The explanation should be no more than three or four sentences. Brief Answers normally refer to the applicable law and key facts upon which the answer is based. If the Memorandum contains multiple Issue Statements, the Brief Answer should respond to those statements in the order in which you posed them, and each brief answer should be a separate paragraph.

D. Statement of Facts

Facts are the grist of the law mill. Readers will not be able to follow your analysis nor assess the strength of your analysis, unless they know the facts upon which you base it. The Statement of Facts orients the reader to the client's situation and should tell a story that pulls together the pertinent facts underlying the dispute. It should arrange the information in an unbiased and readily understandable way.

The Statement of Facts should describe the procedural background of the case and the underlying facts that frame the issue to be discussed. The procedural background paragraph should identify the parties, the nature of the lawsuit or transaction, the relevant procedural moves of the parties, and any court rulings that underlie the issue. Following the procedural background paragraph, the Statement of Facts describes the underlying facts relevant to the issue. The Statement of Facts, therefore, should include all facts analyzed in the Discussion section, as well as background facts necessary for the reader to understand the case. Generally, facts arranged chronologically make for easier reading.

A few other tips. When writing a Statement of Facts, avoid: (1) embellishing or exaggerating the facts; (2) omitting unfavorable facts; or (3) including too many background facts. If citation is necessary, cite accurately to the record, client's statement, deposition, affidavit, or other source. Refer to the parties by their names, rather than as "the plaintiff" or "the defendant."

E. Discussion

In the Discussion section—sometimes called the Analysis—you must analyze the issues that the memo addresses. Like the argument section of a brief, the Discussion should analyze facts based upon the applicable law. Unlike in a brief, however, the Discussion section should objectively analyze the strengths and weaknesses of each argument.

1. Rule Summary

The discussion of each issue should begin with a summary of the applicable law. If the applicable law is based on a constitutional or statutory provision, identify the provision and quote and/or paraphrase the pertinent language of the provision. Then describe the leading precedents, if any, that show how the courts have interpreted the provision. If the applicable law is based on common law, describe how the leading cases have framed the rule. A leading case includes the landmark case that first adopted the rule, a high court's most recent reaffirmation and explanation of the rule, or a precedent that is oft-cited for its thoughtful discussion of the rule. If policy figures in your analysis of your case, describe the policies or purposes the statute or common law rule is intended to further. Most likely, the constitutional, statutory, or common law rule will be composed of two or more elements or factors. Identify these parts of the rule, and define them. A properly constructed rule summary will help you organize the subsequent analysis, by identifying the key parts of the rule, which you will then apply to the facts of your case. Finally, you should note as part of your rule summary any potentially applicable exceptions to the general rule and summarize when the exception applies.

2. Analysis of Facts

You should analyze each element or factor of the rule in light of your case's facts. If an element will be easily established, briefly explain why. If an element will most likely be central to the dispute, your analysis of that element will be longer and present both sides of the argument. For disputed elements, you should define the element and describe precedents, both favorable and unfavorable, that are factually similar to your case. Refrain from describing the facts of precedents that you will not be comparing to your case. Just because you cite a precedent in your memorandum does not mean you must describe it in detail. Some precedents are important because they state the rule clearly and coherently, others because they describe the policy underlying the rule, still others because their facts are sufficiently similar to your case that they can be used to make apt comparisons. When describing a precedent that you will compare with the facts of your case, first state the court's holding. Then briefly describe the key facts of the case. Finally, summarize the court's reasoning: how did the court arrive at its holding?

Once you have described the relevant precedents, you should next actively compare them to your case. Are the precedents analogous to or distinguishable from your case? Explain fully why or why not. What precedents and arguments will most likely be raised by the opposing party? Describe the opposing party's legal position fully. Remember you are drafting an objective document, one that will probably form the basis for future action. You do your client no good by neglecting or sugarcoating the opposing party's potential arguments. Once you have analyzed your client's and the opposing party's arguments, you should weigh those arguments and reach a probable conclusion as to how you think the court will decide the issue. Generally, you should avoid making absolute predictions as to how the court will rule, especially when the opposing party has a plausible legal position.

Sometimes you will have to note the need for additional facts, clarification, or further research; nevertheless, you still should state your conclusion based on the facts and research mentioned in your memorandum.

F. Conclusion

The Conclusion summarizes the Discussion in a more in-depth way than the Brief Answer, but its purpose is essentially the same. The Conclusion should briefly: (1) restate the key issue(s); and (2) offer an opinion as to the likely outcome. Do not include any citations or new arguments (those not mentioned in the Discussion) in the Conclusion. Consider including a recommendation, based on your memorandum's purpose, such as to accept or decline the case, to make or refrain from making a motion, to settle or not settle, to execute or reject the proposed transaction, or to perform further factual investigation or legal research.

G. Headings and Subheadings

Unless your memo is very short, generally you should use subheadings in your Discussion, and possibly your Statement of Facts. Headings and subheadings in memos help the reader understand the logic of the analysis, and enhances readability. Headings in memos should be concise and descriptive. Unlike in persuasive brief writing, headings in memos do not need to be stated as forceful, argumentative conclusions.

Interoffice Memorandum Checklist

Use the following checklists. Go through each step.

Step 1: Formalities

❑ Are you certain about the task? Are you confident about what issue(s) you must discuss?

❑ Do you know the purpose of the memorandum?

❑ What is the deadline?

❑ Who should be copied?

❑ Is there a recommended page limit?

❑ Do you know the facts upon which to base your memorandum?

❑ Will you have to gather facts? Will you need to cite the facts in your memorandum?

❑ Do you know the research parameters for the memorandum (e.g., regulatory law, federal and/or state law, only forum state law, law in other jurisdictions)?

❑ Are there others you can turn to for guidance?

Step 2: The Basics

Next, review the interoffice memo to ensure that it is correct and-complete.

A. The Heading

❑ Do you identify yourself, the intended recipients, and any "cc"s?

❑ Have you dated the memorandum?

❑ Do you have a "Re:" line that accurately describes the topic and the client's identifying number?

B. *Issue Statement and Brief Answer*

❑ Do you have an Issue Statement that states the question that the memorandum answers?

❑ Do you have an Issue Statement for each major issue you are addressing? If you have more than one Issue Statement, is each in a separate paragraph?

❑ If you have two or more Issue Statements, are they in the order in which you analyze them in the Discussion?

❑ Does the Issue Statement identify the rule governing the issue (e.g., negligence, breach of contract)?

❑ Have you stated the Issue Statement objectively and avoided making any legal conclusions?

❑ Does the Issue Statement include a key fact(s) favorable to each party?

❑ Is the Issue Statement one sentence, concisely written, and easily understood?

❑ Do you have a Brief Answer section that immediately follows the Issue Statement section?

❑ Does the Brief Answer directly respond to the Issue Statement and concisely explain why you have reached that answer?

❑ Does the Brief Answer refer to the determinative facts and law upon which the answer is based?

❑ Is the Brief Answer short (i.e., 2–4 short sentences?)

C. *Statement of Facts*

❑ Does your Statement of Facts tell a story that pulls together the pertinent information underlying the case and arranges that information in an unbiased and readily understandable way?

❑ Does the Statement of Facts describe the relevant procedural background of the case?

❑ Is the Statement of Facts accurate, without exaggeration or embellishment?

❏ Does the Statement of Facts include all pertinent facts (those that are analyzed in the Discussion), both favorable and unfavorable to the client?

❏ Is the Statement of Facts supported with accurate citations?

❏ Does the Statement of Facts refer to the parties by their names, rather than, for example, as "plaintiff" or "defendant"?

D. Discussion and Conclusion

❏ Does your Discussion section set forth the applicable law and then analyze the facts based on that law?

❏ Does the Discussion identify the relevant sources of law (e.g., constitutional or statutory provisions, leading cases)?

❏ Does the Discussion identify and define the parts (e.g., elements or factors) of the rule?

❏ Does the Discussion, after the general rule summary, apply the rules to the facts?

❏ Does the Discussion apply each element or factor of the rule to the facts?

❏ Does the Discussion analyze the issue objectively, noting the strengths and weaknesses of the case?

❏ Does the Discussion sufficiently describe comparable precedents (e.g., holding, key facts, rationale)?

❏ Does the Discussion make meaningful, active comparisons between the comparable precedents and the client's case?

❏ Is the Discussion section divided with appropriate headings and sub-headings?

❏ Does the Discussion indicate whether additional facts, clarification, or research may be needed?

❏ Have you cited authority accurately?

❏ Does the Conclusion address the question posed in the Issue Statement? Does the Conclusion identify your opinion as to the likely outcome?

❑ Does the Conclusion summarize the Discussion's analysis in a more in-depth way than the Brief Answer?

❑ Does the Conclusion, if called for, offer a recommended proposed course of action?

* * * * *

Step 3: Now Use the Chapter 1 Checklists to Revise and Improve Your Writing Style

Chapter 6

Letter Writing

Attorneys are prolific letter writers, and letters take a wide variety of forms: from client letters, to formal opinion letters, to engagement letters, to cover letters, to demand letters, to letters of intent, to letters written for discovery purposes. Regardless of their purpose, however, the letters you write convey to your reader the type of lawyer you are. For that reason, they must be clear, well-written, and professional looking.

Letter Writing Fundamentals

Although attorneys write many different kinds of letters, certain fundamentals are common. Law firms, government offices, and corporations will likely all have their own letter templates and format styles that you must follow. But the following describes the basics to writing legal correspondence.

A. Purpose and Audience

Keep in mind your letter's purpose and audience. For a client letter, the purpose may be to convey information and advise your client. Letters written to opposing counsel (e.g., a meet-and-confer or demand letter), on the other hand, may be written with the judge as the ultimate audience. The letter's purpose and intended audience will dictate its content, length, and tone. Always ask: why are you writing this letter, and who is going to read it?

> *"Letters can be extremely effective tools. The first letter sent to a client or adversary often establishes the basis for a relationship. If your letter to adverse counsel is hostile and arrogant, you will be responded to in kind, and this will mark the tone of future communications. You never merely write; you write to someone."*
>
> —Deborah E. Bouchoux, Aspen Handbook for Legal Writers: A Practical Reference 128 (2005).

B. Avoid Legalese

You should avoid legalese, jargon, and other bloated, stuffy expressions when writing a letter. Particularly in letters, lawyers tend to use stock and often arcane phrases. Instead, write in a conversational, business-like, and direct way. Use of elaborate language makes writers look like they are trying too hard to impress.

Examples:

Enclosed herein, please find....	→	I have enclosed....
Pursuant to your request....	→	You asked me to....
Per our agreement....	→	As we agreed....
Your assistance is appreciated.	→	Thank you for your help.
In the above-referenced matter....	→	In this case....

As with other legal writing, avoiding legalese does not mean that you should use colloquialisms or slang.

C. Brevity and Conciseness

Remember that clients, attorneys, and others receiving letters are busy. Letters are most effective when they are no longer than necessary, to the point, and easily understood. Be certain to provide the upshot of your letter (i.e., what you want, or what advice you are giving) at the letter's beginning. Conveying what you want, or summarizing the information you are providing, briefly and clearly at the letter's start, will orient the reader to the letter's purpose.

> *"I apologize for the length of this letter. If I had more time, it would have been shorter."*
>
> —Mark Twain

D. The Paper Trail

Whether you are writing to your client, or to opposing counsel, a primary purpose of letter writing is to leave a paper trail of your work—for example, of advice given, of discovery responses received or not received, of deadlines to be met, and of agreements made. For this reason, letters should be complete, self-contained, and independently understandable (without having to refer to other documents).

E. Proofreading: An Obvious Point

Before sending a letter, always review it one last time for spelling errors, typos, and other mistakes. Letters often create the first impression a client, an opposing counsel, or a judge will have of you. Lawyers often fail to appreciate how much clients and judges read into typos. Many believe that sloppy writing is a tell-tale sign of a sloppy lawyer. When proofreading, ensure that all dates are correct and that you have spelled names (particularly your client's) correctly.

F. The Opening Formalities

Use letterhead for all your legal correspondence. Below your letterhead, include the date and then the recipient's name and address. A common practice is to include a subject or reference (Re:) line below the recipient's address that refers to the letter's topic or subject. Often the subject line will include the case name and the matter involved. A file name may also be included, if appropriate. For example—"Re: Smith v. Jones, Civ. No. 12345—First Request for Production of Documents." After the subject line, place a salutation (e.g., "Dear Ms. Jones:"). Your salutation should end with a colon, not a comma. Usually you should place the salutation two lines below the subject line.

Be certain to identify how you transmitted the letter (e.g., Express Mail, U.S. Mail, Certified Mail, Via Facsimile, etc.) and other special notations (e.g., Attorney-Client Privileged, or Confidential) at the top of the letter. The method of transmittal and other notations should appear below the date, but above the recipient's name and address. *See* Appendix C for examples.

G. Closing and Signature Block

In formal legal correspondence, the closing should be *Sincerely, Sincerely yours, Respectfully,* or something similar, followed by a comma. Avoid informal or intimate closings such as *Humbly yours, Faithfully,* or *Affectionately.* The closing should be one or two lines below the last line of your letter. After the closing, include your signature block. The signature block should consist of your name and possibly your title.

H. Sender/Typist Initials, Enclosures, and Copies

Most letters will indicate the author and typist with the use of initials under the signature block. "AP/mgl" would indicate that Austen Parrish ("AP") authored the letter, but Mark G. Lewis ("mgl") typed it. Place these initials at the left margin one or two lines below the signature block. If you are enclosing something along with the letter, use the word *Enclosure* placed at the left margin, one line below the sender/typist initials. If the letter is sent to a third person, you indicate this by using "cc:" followed by the recipient's name. *See* Appendix C, Sample Letters.

I. Formatting

Legal correspondence should be single-spaced with an extra space (double-space) between paragraphs. Do not double-space your letters as you would do a brief. Twelve point, Times New Roman font is conventional. Number every page of the letter. The convention in legal letters is to indent the first line of each paragraph, and to center the date, closing, and signature block. Consider signing letters in blue ink to easily distinguish originals from photocopies.

* * * * *

> *"All [legal] letters have one thing in common: They are not great literature. They will not be read in a hundred years and analyzed for their wit, charm, or flowery words. With any luck they will be read just once by a few people, followed quickly by their intended result, whether that be compliance, understanding, or agreement."*
>
> —James W. Martin, *How to Write Letters Nonlawyers Will Read* (1999), *available at* www.jamesmartinpa.com

Demand Letters

A demand letter is a letter where an attorney, on behalf of a client, demands that the letter's recipient do something. Demand letters can seek money (e.g., a collection letter) or can demand that the recipient take action (e.g., cease infringing on a client's patent). The following provides some guidelines to writing effective demand letters. An example is also provided in Appendix C.

A. The Tone

Demand letters must sound professional. The letter's tone should be firm and formal, never wishy-washy, rude, or strident. You must assume that eventually a judge may read any letter you write during litigation. For this reason, never overextend or overstate your position, and remove any emotional language. State the facts; do not make unsupported accusations.

B. The First Paragraph

After the opening formalities, introduce yourself, your client, and indicate what you want—i.e., state your demand. Example: "I represent John Smith in connection with his January 1, 2006 accident. I write to demand payment of...."

C. The Factual Summary

In a concise and easy-to-follow description, set forth the key facts upon which you base your demand. The demand letter should include sufficient facts so that the recipients may assess your demand's validity. Be certain that you include all the pertinent facts and state the facts accurately. As with briefs, the factual summary should be stated persuasively and shaded in your client's favor.

D. The Demand

State your client's demand as clearly and succinctly as possible. As part of the demand, describe the legal reasons for the demand: what legally justifies your demand. If you are requesting money, specify the exact amount you seek. If you are requesting that the opposing party take action, be clear what you want that party to do.

E. Expectations and Consequences

Precisely indicate what you want, why you want it, and when you expect compliance. Your demand letter should indicate what options you may pursue if the recipient should ignore your demand. The demand letter should specify what the consequences for compliance and noncompliance will be. Set a specific deadline date so that the recipient knows exactly when you expect compliance with your demand.

F. Be Aware of Legal Pitfalls

Keep in mind the following legal considerations when writing demand letters. First, in some states, demand letters must comply with certain statutory requirements. Be certain you meet those requirements. Second, never correspond directly with someone who is represented by counsel. You violate the codes of legal ethics if you send correspondence directly to a represented party. Third, never threaten criminal prosecution if the letter's recipient fails to comply with the demand. Doing so is unethical and often illegal.

G. How to Send

You must ensure that the demand letter reaches the intended recipient. Send the letter by registered or certified mail so that you can verify that it was received. Before sending—when writing to a business—be certain you know who should receive the demand and put that person's name in the address block. Avoid sending letters simply addressed generally to a corporation.

* * * * *

Opinion Letters

Although there are many types of opinion letters, generally an opinion letter involves the lawyer providing formal written advice to the client on an issue of law. An opinion letter should not abstractly discuss the law. Instead, the opinion letter should answer a client's specific question or address a specific aspect of the client's case that requires the client to make an informed decision. Here are some suggestions for writing opinion letters. An example follows in Appendix C.

A. The Tone

The tone of an opinion letter will differ depending on the type of client. If the client is legally sophisticated, such as a general counsel or an attorney of a corporation's legal department, the tone of your letter will be more sophisticated than if your client has no legal training. For a layperson client, you will have to be careful to explain the law and the potential procedural moves plainly and probably in more detail. For all types of clients, you will have to educate the client about what the law is and how the law affects the client's case and options.

B. The First Paragraph

Give your opinion up front; the client is paying you for your advice. The first paragraph of the letter should: (1) reiterate the client's question; (2) give your legal opinion as to the answer to the question; (3) describe or summarize the legal and factual assumptions upon which you based your opinion; and (4) weave in the critical facts necessary for the opinion.

C. The Factual Summary

After the first paragraph, an opinion letter should set forth the facts upon which you base the opinion. Clients ought to know the specific set of facts you relied upon, and understand that your opinion depends on those facts recited. If the facts turn out to be different, so too may your opinion. Keep the factual summary short, but include all legally significant facts (both favorable and unfavorable) and omit unnecessary detail.

D. The Legal Analysis

After the factual summary, summarize the law upon which you base your opinion. Provide the client with all the information necessary for the client to make an informed decision. Do not just describe the law. Apply the law to the specific facts. In the legal analysis section, the opinion letter is often similar to the analysis section of an interoffice memorandum. Generally, however, the discussion of statutes and cases will be truncated and simplified in the opinion letter. Once you have applied the relevant law, state your conclusions and opinions as clearly and directly as possible.

E. Advice and Caveats

The last part of the opinion letter should recommend a course of action. Do not be overly optimistic in your recommendation, and never provide any guarantee of success. If appropriate, give your client options to consider, and set forth the benefits and drawbacks of each option.

Occasionally, you may lack sufficient information to provide a complete opinion. In those situations, explain what information you need and how your opinion might change given more information. Some firms recommend including a specific caveat indicating that the opinion is based on current law and on the facts currently available.

F. Privileged and Work Product

Before sending out an opinion letter, be absolutely certain that the letter has an appropriate notation or legend that indicates that the opinion letter is work product and attorney-client privileged. You must protect the letter against later discovery.

* * * * *

E-Mails

E-mail is an increasingly common way for attorneys to communicate with their clients, opposing counsel, and others. E-mail also poses unique challenges and risks. Because e-mails are easy to transmit and appear informal, inexperienced attorneys often mistakenly send e-mails inappropriate in tone or content. Because e-mail differs from more traditional legal correspondence, certain caveats are worth bearing in mind.

A. Not as Informal as You May Think

As with other legal correspondence, you should carefully consider your tone and ensure your e-mails are professional. While informal e-mails probably do not need to be meticulously proofread, sending sloppy, poorly-written messages is a mistake. As with other types of writing, e-mails convey the type of attorney you are. Never use text messaging abbreviations (e.g., "BTW"—by the way; "LOL"—laughing out loud; "4u"—for you), or emoticons (e.g., "☺"). Avoid any attempt at humor or sarcasm, as it will often be misunderstood.

B. Discoverable

E-mails may be discoverable. Just because you, or the recipient, deletes an e-mail does not mean that the e-mail no longer exists. Specialized software may be used to retrieve deleted e-mails. Hard copies of the e-mail may exist. Client e-mails mistakenly sent to the wrong recipient may result in the loss of the attorney-client privilege.

When writing client e-mails, you should include an "Attorney-Client Privileged" notation at the very top of the e-mail message. Best practices also dictate that your e-mail indicate that the message is for the recipient named in the message and that if anyone other than the intended recipient receives the e-mail, that person should notify you. Think very carefully whether it would be prudent to send privileged information to your client through e-mail. Does the risk of waiver outweigh the necessity to send the information by e-mail? Do not send sensitive information by e-mail. Remember that once you send the e-mail, you have little control over its distribution. The e-mail can be easily forwarded to others without your knowledge or consent.

C. Short and to the Point

Attorneys and clients, like almost everyone else, receive an enormous amount of e-mail each day. Most people will not read long, rambling messages (or at least will not read them carefully). Keep your e-mail short and focused. E-mails are best used to transmit simple messages or requests. For example, e-mails are useful to schedule, confirm, or cancel meetings, and to convey or ask for contact information or directions.

> *"Lawyers complain that the number of internal messages they receive drains their time and interrupts their other work. Thus think twice before you send an e-mail with a message or question you would not have asked a partner or corporate officer in person or by telephone or interoffice memo."*
>
> —Elizabeth Fajans, et al.,
> Writing for Law Practice 240 (2004).

D. Signatures

An e-mail signature consists of text that is automatically added to the end of an outgoing e-mail message. Consider creating a signature—similar to your business card—with your name, law firm or organization, address, and telephone and facsimile numbers. Another option is to attach a v-card (an electronic business card) to your messages.

E. Professionalism

E-mails should be business-like. Never send or forward inappropriate messages. Lawyers have been disciplined, and even fired, for sending e-mail that contained off-color jokes or inappropriate sexual references, or that ridiculed fellow employees. Triple-check that you are sending the e-mail to the intended recipients. Be careful not to hit by mistake the reply-all button when responding. Doing so may reveal confidential information, or, at minimum, may be embarrassing.

F. Proofread

Clients often complain about the poor quality of the e-mails they receive from their lawyers. Therefore, always spell-check and proofread your e-mail. One problem with proofreading e-mails, compared with other types of correspondence, is that people rarely print out the e-mail to review before sending. The proofing is done on the computer screen. Generally, however, proofreading a hard copy catches more errors. A reader reviewing a hard copy sees the whole page, whereas someone reading an e-mail on a computer screen sees only a fraction of the page. This is why long e-mail messages are especially prone to grammatical and typographical errors, as well as organizational problems. If you must send a long e-mail message, print and review a hard copy before you send it.

G. Formatting

A few formatting suggestions: First, use a standard size, black font (normally 10 point Arial or 11 point Times New Roman) on a white background. E-mails received with unusually large type, decorative fonts, or unexpected color combinations are jarring and difficult to read. Second, for long messages consider preparing the document using a word processor and attaching the document to your e-mail. Word processors generally have greater formatting options and are easier to work with than many e-mail software programs. Third, remember that the e-mail recipient may not have the same software as you do, which could cause the look of your e-mail to change significantly. If the message's format is important, consider converting the message to a PDF file, which preserves the formatting as it appears on your computer screen.

H. Technical Considerations

A few technical considerations: First, consider backing up older, important e-mails. Servers and computers may crash. Second, print out important e-mails for your files. For litigation purposes, you should treat e-mails as you would any other form of correspondence. Third, be careful when using "spam" filters. They may capture or delete important e-mails without your knowledge.

* * * * *

Letter Writing Checklist

Use the following checklist when drafting and revising letters.

Step 1: The Fundamentals

First review the letter for completeness, to ensure that you have all the essential elements of a proper and effective letter.

A. The Opening (the Top of the Letter)

❑ Have you used appropriate letterhead?

❑ Have you dated the letter? Is the date the actual date you are sending the letter? Is it centered?

❑ Have you indicated the method of transmission below the date and above the address line (e.g., via facsimile, first-class mail, certified mail)?

❑ Have you included any necessary notations such as attorney-client privileged or confidential?

❑ Have you made sure that the recipient's name and address are correct?

❑ Do you have a "Re:" line that accurately describes the subject matter of the letter and, if appropriate, your client's identifying number?

❑ Have you used an appropriate salutation followed by a colon?

B. The Body

❑ Does the first paragraph of the letter indicate the letter's purpose? Do you get to the main point right away?

❑ Is the tone of the letter appropriate for the letter's purpose?

❑ Does the letter convey information in a form readily understandable to the recipient? Are you writing the letter to opposing counsel, to the court, or to a legally sophisticated client (e.g., general counsel, co-counsel)? Or is the letter directed to a layperson with little or no legal training?

❑ *Demand Letters:* Are you writing a demand letter?

    ❑ Is the tone firm yet professional?

    ❑ Have you indicated the legal and factual basis for your demand?

    ❑ Have you stated your demand precisely?

    ❑ Have you given a precise deadline for response?

    ❑ Have you indicated the options you may pursue should your demand be ignored or rejected?

❑ *Opinion Letters:* Are you writing an opinion letter for your client?

    ❑ Have you precisely identified the legal question you are addressing in the letter?

    ❑ Have you set forth the relevant facts and law upon which you are basing your opinion?

    ❑ Have you stated your opinion or conclusion clearly?

    ❑ Have you presented your client options that the client should consider?

    ❑ Have you identified any information you may still need to make your opinion more definite?

    ❑ Have you included a caveat that you have based your opinion on current law and the facts as described in the letter?

C. The Close

    ❑ Have you ended the letter with an appropriate closing (e.g., "Sincerely," "Respectfully,") and signature block?

    ❑ Have you included sender/typist initials?

    ❑ If you are including an enclosure, have you made the appropriate notation? If you are including an enclosure, have you made sure that it is actually in the envelope before mailing?

❏ Have you copied (i.e., "cc'd") all necessary persons?

* * * * *

Step 2: Now Use the Chapter 1 Checklists to Revise and Improve Your Writing Style

E-Mail Checklist

Before hitting the "send" button, in addition to following the other tips for effective writing:

❏ Have you kept the e-mail as concise, clear, and as to-the-point as possible?

❏ Is the main point of the e-mail conveyed at the beginning of the message?

❏ Does the message have an appropriate tone? Is it too informal, abrupt, or hostile?

❏ Have you removed any text messaging abbreviations or emoticons?

❏ Is the e-mail professional? Is your message something appropriately said in e-mail? Do you have any concerns for confidentiality that would suggest not sending the message by e-mail?

❏ Have you spell-checked and carefully proofread to remove any typos, spelling mistakes, and grammatical errors?

❏ Have you printed a hard copy of longer e-mails and proofread the hard copy?

❏ Have you triple-checked to ensure that you are not replying to all (if inappropriate to do so), and that you are sending the e-mail to the intended person? Check the e-mail recipient's address again.

❏ Have you included appropriate notations if the e-mail is being sent to a client (e.g., attorney-client privileged and confidential)? Does the e-mail contain an automatic footer to warn against inadvertent disclosure?

❑ Is the e-mail formatted well? Have you considered whether it would be better to send the message either as a word processing document or a PDF file?

❑ Have you used an appropriate e-mail font (usually a black 10 point font against a white background)?

❑ Have you included an e-mail signature or v-card that includes your name and relevant contact information?

Chapter 7

Academic Writing

For law students, completing well-written seminar papers, student comments, or case notes is necessary to excel in upper division seminar courses and to publish with law journals. But academic writing is important beyond law school. Strong academic writing can help you obtain a job. At the very least, a published article enhances your résumé. And increasingly lawyers write academic papers as a means of advancing their careers, garnering respect within the profession, and contributing to their field. Having a well-written article published can be a way for a junior attorney to attract clients and impress senior attorneys.

The following advice distills some basic principles for how practicing attorneys can write and publish a law review article. These techniques work equally well for law students writing comments, notes, or seminar papers.[1]

---

1. An in-depth discussion of all the ins and outs of scholarly writing is beyond this book's scope. For a detailed discussion of scholarly writing, two good books are: EUGENE VOLOKH, ACADEMIC LEGAL WRITING: LAW REVIEW ARTICLES, STUDENT NOTES, SEMINAR PAPERS, AND GETTING ON LAW REVIEW (2d ed. 2005); and ELIZABETH FAJANS & MARY R. FALK, SCHOLARLY WRITING FOR LAW STUDENTS: SEMINAR PAPERS, LAW REVIEW NOTES, AND LAW REVIEW COMPETITION PAPERS (3d ed. 2005).

Approach and Preparation

Although academic writing can take several forms, including law review articles, case comments, book reviews, and practitioner guides, the approach to writing each of them is generally the same.

A. Find a Topic

Your interests and practice areas are logical starting places in finding a topic. It helps, but is not essential, to pick a topic with which you have some prior experience, since your learning curve will not be as steep. Attending conferences, symposia, or continuing-legal-education seminars is a good way to hear about interesting topics worth writing about. So too are having conversations with colleagues working on "cutting edge" cases and, of course, with your former and current professors. Other sources to consider include: (1) newspapers, both national and local; (2) legal periodicals, such as law reviews, bar journals, legal newspapers, and recent additions to the Index to Legal Periodicals; (3) advance sheets; and (4) casebooks (review the question and note sections that follow landmark cases). Keep in mind that unless you enjoy researching and writing for their own sake, you should choose a topic that will hold your interest for many weeks and even months: writing a law review article takes time, probably more time than you think. To make the project manageable, you should focus on a specific and narrow topic, rather than a broad one.

> "[F]ind one new point, one new insight, one new way of looking at a piece of law, and organize your entire article around that. One insight from another discipline, one application of simple logic to a problem where it has never been made before is all you need."
>
> —Richard Delgado, *How to Write a Law Review Article*, 20 U.S.F. L. Rev. 445, 448 (1986).

B. Develop a Thesis

Once you have picked a topic, you need to develop a thesis. Your thesis should be an original, plausible, and useful insight into your article's topic. Potential theses include describing how courts have formulated, interpreted, and applied a particular legal doctrine, identifying and solving a legal problem, explaining a legal phenomenon in a novel way (perhaps by taking an inter-disciplinary approach), uncovering previously unknown influences underlying legal milestones, or developing a new theoretical framework for a major legal doctrine. Your thesis can be modest. In fact, for your first scholarly article, focusing on an easily managed thesis is a wise choice. Avoid a thesis that contributes nothing new, since it will have no use to the profession — in other words, do not write an article just for the sake of writing an article. Unless you are writing a how-to-guide, your thesis should be a novel way of solving, or a novel way of viewing, a legal problem.

> *"Good legal scholarship should make (1) a claim that is (2) novel, (3) nonobvious, (4) useful, (5) sound, and (6) seen by the reader to be novel, nonobvious, useful, and sound. This is true whether the author is a student, a young lawyer, a seasoned expert, or an academic."*
>
> —Eugene Volokh, Academic Legal Writing: Law Review Articles, Student Notes, Seminar Papers, and Getting on Law Review 9 (2d ed. 2005).

C. Set a Schedule

Of all the types of legal writing, academic writing is the most time-consuming. Writing a law review article presents significant time management challenges; indeed, writing even a relatively short descriptive essay for a bar journal can seem a daunting task. Law review articles are often 50–60 pages or longer, contain extensive footnotes, and involve in-depth legal analysis. Therefore, you should set deadlines for completing an outline, first draft, second draft, etc. A well-researched, developed article may take six months or longer to write. Ideally, set aside some time each day to work on your article. And keep to your schedule.

D. Conduct a Thorough Preemption-Check

As with other writing projects, start your research by consulting secondary sources (e.g., treatises, legal encyclopedias, law review or bar journal articles). Reading recently published law review articles can also help you narrow down your topic. You will need an overview of the area of law that you are writing about. After doing so, look for articles that address or touch on your topic. You should consult, at minimum: (1) the Index to Legal Periodicals; (2) the Law Review/Journal databases from Westlaw and Lexis; (3) the book catalogues of local law libraries; and (4) the Social Science Research Network (www.ssrn.com) for unpublished articles. You must survey what has previously been written not only because those articles will be useful in developing and refining your thesis, but to ensure that your thesis has not been preempted (i.e., someone has already written on the same topic with the same or very similar thesis as yours). If your article lacks novelty, law reviews will have no reason to publish it. Keep a list of all sources consulted, and articles read, during your preemption check. If all goes well, you will have developed a novel thesis.

E. Thoroughly Research

You must be fluent with the literature surrounding your topic. In other words, you must thoroughly research and assimilate that research into your understanding and development of the topic. The scope of your research will be guided by your topic. Is your topic a national issue or does it pertain to a particular state? Does your article resolve a split among the jurisdictions? Do you analyze your topic from a social science perspective? Does your article take a comparative law approach? Your research will have to reflect the breadth of your topic. That is why articles are much easier to manage when they are narrower in scope. Even with seemingly narrow topics, you may well be surprised at how much you need to research. Are you examining an issue of your own state law? You will have to research the evolution of your state law and the problems caused by that law. Additionally, your research may well extend beyond your own state law. If you are suggesting a solution to the problem, you may well need to determine how other jurisdictions deal with the issue, which would greatly expand your research universe.

F. Write Your Introduction/Free-Writing

Once you have a handle on the research, start writing. Two approaches recommend themselves. One approach is to draft your Introduction first. By doing so, you will have a synopsis of your article. Some find writing the Introduction provides an anchor upon which to write a substantial outline and a draft. If you use this approach, you should expect your Introduction to change significantly—do not become wed to your initial draft of the Introduction. Another approach is to free-write, or what some colorfully refer to as "dump drafting." With this approach, you "dump" on the page all of your thoughts about your thesis, without regard for organization, clarity, or writing style. This approach promotes creativity, by getting ideas down on paper quickly. You will later work on organization and readability.

G. Outline and Write Out Headings

Your next step is to develop a detailed outline of your article. Outlining is an important step to help you develop the thesis and organize your points logically and forcefully. If you wrote a "dump draft," cull through it to spot related issues and points, and create order from the chaos. Group related points or categories of points, and begin drafting headings. As with briefs, by writing out your headings, you force yourself to think through the article's structure. When outlining, consider listing under each heading the key articles, cases, and other authority that you intend to discuss.

If you dislike detailed outlining, at least make a list of subtopics or chart out your notes and research to keep yourself organized. If you fail to think through the article's basic structure early on in the writing process, you will almost certainly waste significant time later on.

H. Multiple Drafts

After completing your outline and tentative headings, the time has come to write a complete rough draft. Completing your first draft is a separate step from rewriting, revising, editing, and polishing. The key is to complete the draft—no matter how rough. Since you have your outline, begin anywhere you want. No need exists to start at the beginning and work through to the article's end. Instead, just write and get something down on paper.

You should expect to write many drafts—perhaps ten, twenty, or more—depending on the article's complexity, your experience with academic writing, and the time you can spend on the article. The idea is to take your first rough draft and revise it multiple times to arrive at a solid draft that you can then systematically edit. As you revise your drafts, ask: Have you fully developed your thesis? Does your analysis lead logically to your conclusion? Have you included all important issues? Is your research complete? Have you discussed the key cases, statutes, and scholarly articles that are relevant to your topic? Have you accurately described the law? Is each section fully developed and internally coherent?

I. Edit Systematically

Once you have transformed your first draft into a substantively sound, complete draft, you need to begin the editing process. Use the editing checklists from Chapter 1 to systematically edit your writing. Editing requires going through your article sentence by sentence, carefully correcting mistakes and improving writing style. As with other kinds of legal writing, you can not possibly do everything at once. Instead, you should edit the article in bite-size chunks (e.g., section by section, or paragraph by paragraph).

J. Rewrite Your Introduction and Conclusion

Once you have finished editing and you are satisfied with the body of the article, you should return to your Introduction and Conclusion and rewrite them. Sound reasons support this practice. First, the article may have changed in tone or focus by virtue of your editing. Once you have finished editing, your view of your thesis often has changed (not surprisingly, since you will have a deeper understanding of the issues than when you started). Second, the Introduction is by far the article's most important part. Lawyers, professors, and others coming across your article are busy. Many readers may initially read only the Introduction. You must give readers a reason to read on: a well-written, provocative introduction will catch their attention and pull them deeper into your article (see the section below on Introductions for tips on how to do this). Rewrite your Conclusion too, to ensure that you have captured the highlights of the points you made in the article.

K. Proofread and Polish

Careful proofreading is critical. Typos, spelling mistakes, and other errors reflect badly on you and the article, and can reduce your chances of having your article published. Here are two reminders: First, you will want to proofread from a hard copy, not from the computer screen; spotting errors is generally easier this way. Second, proofreading is a separate process from editing. When proofreading the article, consider placing a straight-edge ruler under each line as you read. Doing so forces you to focus on each line and should help you catch mistakes. Alternatively, read the article slowly out loud, focusing on each word to catch errors. You have not finished the article—and should not send it out for review—until you have proofread it several times.

* * * * *

Law Review Article Fundamentals

Law review articles (and other types of academic writing) have certain common features. Here are some fundamentals to help you draft a sound law review article.

A. The Title

Writing a good title is a challenge. A good title will be descriptive, so that the reader can at a glance get a sense of the article's point. Your title must be easy to understand, and you should take care to make your title clear, direct, and relatively short. A memorable title will help with placing your article and getting it read. Avoid abstract titles containing legal jargon or obscure references. Avoid citations to cases or to statutes in your article's title. Many writers often use a very short main title, followed by a longer, more descriptive subtitle.[2]

B. Introduction

Never underestimate the importance of a readable, striking Introduction. While your Introduction should provide a roadmap of what is to come, an Introduction should not merely summarize. The Introduction should be provocative and forceful, encouraging people to read further. The Introduction should: (1) describe the legal problem you are addressing; (2) state and summarize your thesis or solution to the legal problem; and (3) provide a roadmap of the article's structure. You must make these points concisely, while also capturing the reader's attention. Good introductions usually require only a few pages.

C. Background

The background section is where you provide necessary information for the reader to understand, and for you to prove, your thesis. Your background section should fully describe the legal problem you are addressing. Here, you will lay the foundation for your thesis by

---

2. Here are two examples of titles, from the authors' own works: Austen L. Parrish, *Sovereignty, Not Due Process: Personal Jurisdiction Over Nonresident Alien Defendants*, 41 WAKE FOREST L. REV. 1 (2006); Dennis T. Yokoyama, *You Can't Always Use the* Zippo *Code: The Fallacy of a Uniform Theory of Internet Personal Jurisdiction*, 54 DePaul L. REV. 1147 (2005).

describing applicable legal doctrines and policies central to your topic. The background section should be relatively short: your thesis, not your summary of existing law, is your contribution to legal knowledge. Limit the background section only to those matters (be it constitutional or statutory provisions, cases, history of legal doctrines, competing policies, disadvantages of current doctrine, etc.) that are essential to establishing your thesis. For many articles, you will need to discuss the existing law. Avoid detailed discussions of individual cases, when the discussions do not aid in proving or disproving your thesis or are otherwise redundant. You should resist discussing every case or issue simply because it is there; discuss only those things critical to developing your thesis.

D. Analysis: Explore Your Thesis

Your analysis section is where you establish your thesis—the focus of the article. Keep the following suggestions in mind when drafting your Analysis section. First, use policy to show that your approach to the legal problem is the best one. You have already, in your background section, identified the disadvantages of the current legal doctrine. Explain why the impact of those disadvantages necessitates a new approach, your proposed solution. Explain how your solution minimizes or eliminates the disadvantages and how your solution advances significant public policies. Second, identify and respond to any potential weaknesses or obvious counterarguments to your position. Third, be certain to use the right tone. As with other legal writing, address the points made by others but refrain from personalizing your arguments or personally attacking those with whom you disagree. Lastly, try to connect your thesis to the broader academic debates surrounding your topic. By doing so, you make your thesis more useful to academics, and thus they are more likely to cite your article.

E. Headings and Subheadings

Divide both your background and analysis sections with headings and subheadings. Headings permit a reader to easily follow your article's structure and hence the logic of your thesis. For this reason, write descriptive headings and subheadings that identify and advance specific arguments, rather than generic headings (e.g., "Background," "The Law," or "The Analysis"). As with briefs, your headings and subheadings alone should provide a clear and logical roadmap or outline of your analysis—the building blocks upon which you base and develop your thesis. Of course, you can have too much of a good thing. Too many subheadings will make your writing stilted and interrupt the writing's flow. Do not use short subsections (e.g., less than a double-spaced page).

F. Conclusion

Unlike in a brief, a Conclusion in a law review article is substantive. It should be short, forceful, and direct, while reminding the reader of the key contributions your article makes. Avoid merely summarizing your points in the Conclusion. Instead, use the Conclusion to highlight and explain the significance of your most important points.

> "[T]he best conclusions end with a bang, not a whimper. As your last word on the topic, conclusions tend to be remembered, and thus deserve special crafting ... Mere summary is anti-climactic ... [L]eave the reader excited about the subject matter and interested in exploring it further."
>
> —Elizabeth Fajans & Mary R. Falk,
> Scholarly Writing for Law Students 138–39 (3d ed. 2005).

G. The Abstract

In submitting your article for publication, you should include a short abstract. The abstract should usually be less than 500 words long. Think of the abstract as a mini-Introduction of your article. Thus your abstract must grab the reader's attention, emphasize the significance of your thesis, and encourage the reader to read on.

H. Table of Contents

Include a Table of Contents with your article. The Table of Contents should identify each section of the article and provide corresponding page numbers. Drafting a Table of Contents serves at least two purposes. First, setting up and modifying the Table of Contents as you revise and edit your article focuses your attention on your article's structure and organization. Second, a Table of Contents provides the reader with an overview of the article at a glance, enabling readers to turn quickly to the parts of the article that interest them.

I. Citations

In law review articles, all citations to authority should appear in footnotes. Most law reviews do not accept articles with endnotes, and—unlike the convention for legal briefs—authority is never cited within the text. You should footnote all assertions of law, fact, or opinion. Most law reviews require footnotes to follow citation formats set forth by the *Bluebook* or the *ALWD Citation Manual*. Avoid long, talking, or textual footnotes. Footnotes should be used for listing authority relied upon, not for long, tangential discussions of the material in the text. Long textual footnotes can be distracting and interrupt the article's flow. Before sending an article out for publication consideration, you should ensure that each authority in every footnote is properly cited.

J. Do Not Plagiarize

Plagiarism is the passing off of another person's work as one's own, or without proper attribution. When you write a law review article, you must indicate where you got your information. If you use the work of others, quote their words, or paraphrase their ideas, acknowledge and cite their work in a footnote.

* * * * *

Getting Published

If you have a well-written article with an interesting thesis, law reviews will want to publish it. Although strategies abound for getting published, here are some suggestions.

A. Formatting and Length

Your article should look like a published article. Do not send out an incomplete draft. Do not send out articles that are double, or triple-spaced. Your article should be book-formatted—single-spaced with formatted headings and justified margins. The conventional font for text is an 11 or 12 point Times, New Century Schoolbook, or other serifed typeface font. Footnotes should be in a smaller font (e.g., 10 point). Ensure that you have cited all footnotes properly. In recent years, law reviews from many schools (e.g., Harvard, Yale, Stanford) prefer articles under 25,000 words long. Lengthy articles (over 100 pages) are difficult, if not impossible, to place.

B. Reviews and Comments

Before submitting your article for publication consideration, you should send the article to friends and colleagues to review and provide comments. If possible, solicit comments from academics who have written in the field. Also consider posting your article on the Social Science Research Network (www.ssrn.com). This is a free service that allows you to publicize and solicit comments about the article prior to its publication.

C. Cover Letter and Résumé

When submitting your article and the abstract, you should include a cover letter. The cover letter should be attention-grabbing, and quickly explain why your article is thoughtful and original. Cover letters should generally be no more than one or two pages long. As with the Introduction section of your article, the cover letter is your opportunity to sell your paper. Attach your résumé or curriculum vitae to the cover letter.

D. Submission Timing

Timing is critical: you should submit articles to law reviews in one of two time periods. The first period begins in early March with the appointment of the new student editorial board. The second begins in late August when the student editors return to law school. Avoid submitting any articles from October through February, or April through early August. Journals usually fill up for the year by late March and again in late September. Submitting outside these windows of time will mean your article probably will not be read, and thus will not be published.

> "It is absolutely crucial that authors submit articles during the two recognized seasons, Spring season and Fall season.... Submitting an article in December is the functional equivalent of dropping it off a bridge."
>
> —Kaimipono Wenger, *Publishing Your Work in Law Reviews: Tips On How To Get Your Article Published, available at* www.law.columbia.edu.

E. Where to Submit

You should submit your article to the main journals of at least 20–30 law schools and to several relevant specialty journals. Submitting an article to a hundred law reviews for publication consideration, however, is not unusual, and may well be the common practice. Many resources exist to help you decide which law reviews to submit to. Washington & Lee Law School has a comprehensive ranking of law reviews based on citation counts (http://lawlib.wlu.edu/LJ/index .aspx). This webpage has address and contact information for most law reviews in the United States and Canada. Emory Law School also has contact information for the most well-regarded law reviews (http://www.law.emory.edu/library/alpharevlimits. html), as does the Jurist webpage (http://jurist.law.pitt.edu/lawreviews), and Lexis/Nexis.

F. How to Submit

You principally have three options for submitting. First, Berkeley Electronic Press has an online service, known as ExpressO, that will allow you to electronically submit your article to over 450 journals. The cost is reasonable, and ExpressO permits you to upload your article, cover letter, and résumé. Second, you can manually print and mail a copy of your article (and supporting documents) directly to the journal. Many journals will allow you to submit the article by e-mail. E-mail addresses can easily be obtained from individual law review webpages, and from the Washington & Lee rankings. Third, many law reviews have their own webpages, and prefer that you upload articles directly to those sites (e.g., Columbia Law Review, Georgetown Law Journal, Harvard Law Review, Stanford Law Review, and the Yale Law Journal, among others).

G. The Expedited Review Process

Once you receive an offer from a law journal for your article, you will want to do two things. First, confirm the terms of the offer and the date on which the offer will expire. Generally, law journals will give you between a week and two weeks to accept an offer. Second, request an expedited review (i.e., a publication decision before the deadline) from other journals that you remain interested in publishing with. Make your request both by telephone, and by e-mail. Some highly-ranked law reviews generally do not read articles until they have received an expedited review request. In your e-mail requesting an expedited review, include: (1) your name and contact information; (2) the name of the law review that has given you the offer; and (3) the impending deadline. Also attach an electronic copy of your manuscript to the e-mail. You want to make it as easy as possible for the student editors to read your article.

* * * * *

Academic Writing Checklist

Use the following checklist when drafting and revising articles.

Step 1: The Fundamentals

A. The Title and Introduction

❑ Is your title descriptive, easy to understand, and memorable?

❑ Have you avoided using an abstract, obscure, or jargon-filled title?

❑ Is your Introduction attention grabbing?

❑ Does your Introduction describe the legal problem you are addressing?

❑ Does your Introduction state and summarize your thesis or solution to the legal problem?

❑ Does your Introduction provide a roadmap of the article's structure?

❑ Is your Introduction no more than a few pages long?

B. Background

❑ Have you created the foundation upon which your thesis is based? Have you described the relevant legal doctrines, policies, and history that are central to your topic?

❑ Is your Background limited to those matters that are essential to establishing your thesis?

❑ Have you avoided detailed discussions of individual cases, unless necessary for your thesis?

C. Your Thesis, Analysis, and Conclusion

❑ Is your analysis broken up with an appropriate number of headings and subheadings?

❑ Are your headings and subheadings descriptive?

❑ Have you explained why your thesis is the best approach to a legal problem? Have you fully supported your thesis?

❑ Have you responded to obvious counter-arguments or weaknesses in your position?

❑ Have you responded or referred to key articles and works in the field? Have you connected your thesis to broader debates occurring in academia?

❑ Have you refrained from personally attacking those with whom you disagree?

❑ Have you avoided merely summarizing your article in the conclusion?

❑ Do you have a substantive conclusion? Is it short, yet forceful? Have you highlighted the key points your article makes?

*   *   *   *   *

Step 2: Now Use the Chapter 1 Checklists to Revise and Improve Your Writing Style

Appendix A

Recommended Reading and Selected Bibliography

A. Grammar and Style Manuals

- Deborah E. Bouchoux, *Aspen Handbook for Legal Writers: A Practical Reference* (2005)
- Anne Enquist & Laurel Currie Oates, *Just Writing: Grammar, Punctuation, and Style for the Legal Writer* (2d ed. 2005)
- Ian Gallacher, *A Form and Style Manual for Lawyers* (2005)
- Bryan A. Garner, *Legal Writing in Plain English: A Text with Exercises* (2001)
- Bryan A. Garner, *The Redbook: A Manual on Legal Style* (2d ed. 2006)
- William Strunk Jr. & E.B. White, *The Elements of Style* (4th ed. 2000)
- Richard C. Wydick, *Plain English for Lawyers* (5th ed. 2005)

B. Legal Writing Generally

- Gertrude Block, *Effective Legal Writing for Law Students and Lawyers* (5th ed. 1999)
- Charles R. Calleros, *Legal Method and Writing* (5th ed. 2006)
- Bradley G. Clary & Pamela Lysaght, *Successful Legal Analysis and Writing: The Fundamentals* (2d ed. 2006)

- Linda H. Edwards, *Legal Writing and Analysis* (2d ed. 2007)
- Michael D. Murray & Christy H. DeSanctis, *Legal Research and Writing* (2005)
- Richard K. Neumann, Jr., *Legal Reasoning and Legal Writing: Structure, Strategy, and Style* (5th ed. 2005)
- Mary Barnard Ray, *The Basics of Legal Writing* (2006)
- Jane N. Richmond, *Legal Writing: Form & Function* (2002)
- Helene S. Shapo, et al., *Writing and Analysis in the Law* (4th rev. ed. 2003)
- Louis J. Sirico & Nancy Schultz, *Legal Writing and Other Lawyering Skills* (4th ed. 2004)
- Robin Wellford Slocum, *Legal Reasoning, Writing, and Persuasive Argument* (2d ed. 2006).

C. Brief Writing, Appellate Practice, and Oral Advocacy

- Ruggero J. Aldisert, *Winning On Appeal: Better Briefs and Oral Argument* (2003)
- Mary Beth Beazley, *A Practical Guide to Appellate Advocacy* (2d ed. 2006)
- Carole C. Berry, *Effective Appellate Advocacy: Brief Writing and Oral Argument* (3d ed. 2003)
- Maria L. Ciampi & William H. Manz, *The Question Presented: Model Appellate Briefs* (2000)
- Bradley G. Clary, et al., *Advocacy On Appeal* (2d ed. 2004)
- David C. Frederick, *The Art of Oral Advocacy* (2003)
- Michael D. Murray & Christy H. DeSanctis, *Appellate Advocacy and Moot Court* (2006)
- *Introduction to Advocacy* (David Ware, et al., eds. 7th ed. 2002)
- Laurel Currie Oates & Anne Enquist, *Just Briefs* (2002)

- Theresa J. Reid Rambo & Leanne J. Pflaum, *Legal Writing by Design: A Guide to Great Briefs and Memos* (2001)
- Michael R. Smith, *Advanced Legal Writing: Theories and Strategies in Persuasive Writing* (2002)
- Steven D. Stark, *Writing to Win: The Legal Writer* (1999)

D. Legal Memorandum and Letters

- John Bronsteen, *Writing a Legal Memo* (2006)
- Laurel Currie Oates & Anne Enquist, *Just Memos* (2d ed. 2006)
- Elizabeth Fajans, et al., *Writing for Law Practice* (2004)

E. Academic Writing

- Elizabeth Fajans & Mary R. Falk, *Scholarly Writing for Law Students: Seminar Papers, Law Review Notes, and Law Review Competition Papers* (3d ed. 2005)
- Eugene Volokh, *Academic Legal Writing: Law Review Articles, Student Notes, Seminar Papers, and Getting on Law Review* (2d ed. 2005)

F. Other

- Mark Hermann, *How to Write: A Memorandum from a Curmudgeon*, 24 No. 1 Litigation 3 (Fall 1997)
- Wilson Huhn, *The Five Types of Legal Argument* (2002)
- Margaret Z. Johns, *Professional Writing for Lawyers: Skills and Responsibilities* (1998)
- Joseph Kimble, *Lifting the Fog of Legalese: Essays on Plain Language* (2005)
- Brad Wendel, *Matters of Style: A Cranky Opinionated Guide* (2002).
- Scott Wood, *Practical Persuasion: A Writing Workshop* (2002)

Appendix B

Sample Briefs

Sample Introductions to Briefs

Example #1:

The following is an Introduction to a California trial court brief, where the defendant seeks leave to file a cross-complaint.

> **INTRODUCTION**
>
> At the heart of ABC Corporation's Complaint are contested allegations that XYZ, Inc. breached a contract involving the sale of cellular telephone service, when XYZ allegedly failed to pay commissions allegedly owed under that contract. In fact, XYZ overpaid commissions, and ABC owes XYZ more than $1 million. XYZ now brings this motion for leave to file a compulsory cross-complaint against ABC to recover those commissions.
>
> California law strongly favors granting leave to file compulsory claims. A motion for leave to file a compulsory cross-complaint may be denied *only if* substantial evidence of the movant's bad faith exists. Here, the Court should grant XYZ's motion because: (1) XYZ's Cross-Complaint states a compulsory claim as it arises from the same operative facts underlying ABC's Complaint—the payment of commissions arising under the contract; (2) far from acting in bad faith, XYZ diligently prepared its Cross-Complaint immediately after the court lifted the stay pending appeal; and (3) ABC will suffer no prejudice from the granting of this motion, while XYZ will suffer great harm if the court denies it.

The writer begins the trial court brief's first paragraph by: (1) introducing who the parties are; and (2) quickly explaining why the defendant is before the court (i.e., what the motion is about and the specific request).

In the second paragraph—in a crisp, concise style—the writer summarizes why the court should grant the motion. Even if the judge reads only this Introduction, the judge will know the basic grounds upon which relief is requested.

> Moreover, the granting of XYZ's motion will not effect a delay in this litigation. No trial date has been set, and leave would not delay the completion of discovery since XYZ's Cross-Complaint is premised on the very same facts and occurrences that are the subject of ABC's Complaint and XYZ's affirmative defenses. Accordingly, the Court should grant XYZ's Motion for Leave to File a Cross-Complaint.

Notice how the Introduction embraces some of the writing techniques discussed.

- The writer uses the active voice (e.g., instead of "XYZ's Motion for Leave to File a Cross-Complaint should be granted" the writer focuses on the actor—"the Court should grant….").

- The writer avoids an unnecessary preposition, and instead opts for possessive constructions (e.g., "XYZ's Cross-Complaint" instead of "the Cross-Complaint of XYZ.").

- The writer uses transitions to connect sentences (e.g., "In fact," "Here," "Moreover," and "Accordingly").

- The writer varies sentence length and utilizes a list beginning with a colon and separated by semicolons. The number of words in each sentence is: 35, 13, 18, 10, 22, 79, 14, 38, and 13.

- The Introduction concludes with a specific request for relief.

* * * * *

Example #2:

Below is an Introduction (here titled "Preliminary Statement") to a brief opposing a Petition for a Writ of Supersedeas before a California appellate court.

PRELIMINARY STATEMENT

This Petition for Writ of Supersedeas is Appellant and Judgment Debtor ABC's latest attempt to delay and avoid payment of approximately $5.8 million it owes to Respondent and Judgment Creditor XYZ Financial Corporation. ABC owes this money pursuant to a Deficiency Judgment that the court entered against ABC personally. Upon filing his appeal, ABC did not petition for a writ of supersedeas. Instead, six months later—after repeatedly delaying the appeal—ABC has suddenly requested a stay, stating that if its petition is not immediately granted it will suffer irreparable harm. But there is no basis for the extraordinary relief sought, and this Court should reject ABC's latest dilatory tactic.

This Court should deny ABC's Petition for Writ of Supersedeas for several reasons. *First*, ABC's appeal is meritless because it is based on the frivolous argument that a deficiency judgment is not a judgment, but a "supplemental enforcement order." ABC's argument— which ignores the plain language of the Civil Procedure Code and controlling en banc Supreme Court authority—was rejected by three trial judges in two courts below, and should be summarily rejected here too. *Sec-*

The writer begins the brief by: (1) introducing who the parties are; and (2) summarizing the dispute. At the end of the first paragraph, the writer identifies the requested relief.

The second paragraph—starting with a clear topic sentence— summarizes why the court should grant the petition. Bold/Italics are used sparingly—only to aid the court in identifying the three reasons to grant the petition.

> **ond**, after waiting six months to file this petition, ABC does not and can not make the showing of irreparable harm necessary to grant the extraordinary relief it requests. **Third**, it is black-letter law that an appeal from an order denying a motion to vacate, as ABC has made here, will not stay enforcement of a money judgment.
>
> Under these circumstances, the Court should deny ABC's request for a stay. If this Court is inclined to enter a stay, XYZ respectfully requests that the Court impose reasonable conditions on the stay by requiring that ABC post an appropriate bond.

* * * * *

This Introduction also embraces the writing techniques explained in this Handbook.

- The writer varies sentence length, but the sentences are relatively short. The sentence lengths are: 33, 16, 13, 9, 20, 13, 26, 36, 29, 30, 12, and 29.

- The writer uses the active voice (e.g., "the Court should....").

- The writer avoids nominalizations, and instead opts for possessive constructions (e.g., "ABC's Petition....")

- The writer signposts his or her arguments ("First ... Second ... Third....").

- The Introduction concludes with a specific request for relief.

Sample Appellate Brief

Below are excerpts from an Appellate Brief that one of the authors wrote for a case before a California appellate court.

2nd Civil No. **B168175**

IN THE

COURT OF APPEAL

FOR THE

STATE OF CALIFORNIA
SECOND APPELLATE DISTRICT
DIVISION THREE

Jamal B., *Plaintiff and Appellant*

v.

County of Los Angeles et al., *Defendant and Respondent.*

APPEAL FROM THE SUPERIOR COURT OF THE COUNTY OF LOS ANGELES
THE HONORABLE HELEN I. BENDIX, JUDGE
CIVIL CASE No. BC 260156

APPLICATION OF PUBLIC COUNSEL FOR LEAVE TO FILE *AMICUS CURIAE* BRIEF; *AMICUS CURIAE* BRIEF IN SUPPORT OF APPELLANT JAMAL B.

AUSTEN L. PARRISH (S.B. No. 194198)
SOUTHWESTERN UNIVERSITY
SCHOOL OF LAW
675 S. Westmoreland Ave.
Los Angeles, CA 90005-3992
(213) 738-5728

PAUL L. FREESE, JR. (S.B. No. 139133)
LESLIE A. PARRISH (S.B. No. 195861)
Children's Rights Project
PUBLIC COUNSEL
601 S. Ardmore Avenue
Los Angeles, CA 90005
(213) 385-2977

Attorneys for Amicus Curiae Public Counsel

The Cover Page is clean, professional looking, and without spelling or grammatical errors. First impressions are important.

QUESTIONS PRESENTED

1. Even if a county has not violated a mandatory, statutory duty, may a county be held derivatively liable, under Government Code section 815.2(a), for its social worker's negligent failure to remove a disabled child from a placement known to be inappropriate and dangerous?

2. Does a trial court err in granting. . . .

One of the two Questions Presented from this brief is included here. Notice how the Question Presented: (1) is one sentence long; (2) identifies a specific body of law; and (3) includes facts specific to the case (i.e. "disabled child," "placement known to be inappropriate and dangerous," and "when the county admits").

* * * * *

TABLE OF CONTENTS

Immediately following the Questions Presented is the Table of Contents. The Table of Contents should allow a judge to follow quickly the logic of the Argument.

Absent from the Table of Contents is underlining, bold, or italics.

Notice how each Point Heading is an independent, separate reason for why the Court should grant the requested relief.

The writer has framed each Point Heading as focusing on why the lower court erred.

STATEMENT OF THE CASE

I. Summary Of Material Facts

Appellant Jamal B. is a disabled child, who is a paraplegic and suffers from significant development disabilities. (JA 120:19–22.) Jamal has been under the County's Department of Child and Family Services' care and supervision since birth. (JA 121:1–3, 9–16; 722:14–21.) He was removed from his natural parents' home, when he was less than two months old, because his natural parents were unable to care for him. (JA 120:23–27.) The County placed Jamal in Wilene Douglas's home, as a foster-care child. (JA 121:1–3.) Although Douglas later became Jamal's legal guardian, Jamal always remained under the County's supervision and control. (JA 121:4–16, 691:2–9.) Douglas received money from the County because of Jamal's special needs. (*Id.*)

That the County had a duty to supervise and monitor Jamal is undisputed. Indeed, the County embraces this duty. (JA 163:6–17, 556:25–26.) * * * *

Here is a short excerpt from the Statement of the Case. In this brief, the writer chose to discuss the factual record before describing the procedural posture of the case.

Notice how in the first paragraph the writer introduces the parties. After each sentence is a record cite to the Joint Appendix. The record citations are set-off by parentheticals to avoid distracting the Court or interrupting the sentence flow.

STANDARD OF REVIEW

The primary issue on appeal is solely a question of law: whether a county is entitled to immunity for its social worker's alleged negligent acts. (*Barner v. Leeds* (2000) 24 Cal.4th 676, 683 [determining discretionary act immunity as a question of law after the trial court granted summary judgment].) This Court's review is therefore de novo. (*Id.; see also Stout v. City of Porterville* (1983) 148 Cal.App.3d 937, 941 ["The existence of a duty is entirely a question of law...."].) Of course, this is an appeal from a summary judgment, which itself requires de novo review. (*Merrill v. Navegar, Inc.* (2001) 26 Cal.4th 465, 476; *Buss v. Superior Court* (1997) 16 Cal.4th 35, 60.) Accordingly, all doubts as to the propriety of granting summary judgment must be resolved in Jamal's favor. (*Saelzler v. Advanced Group 400* (2001) 25 Cal.4th 763, 768.)

The brief-writer summarizes the Standard of Review, with citation to binding authority. The writer refers back to the Standard of Review throughout the brief.

The citations in this brief follow California style requirements. Notice how each citation contains a pinpoint cite, so that the Court may easily find the cited material.

ARGUMENT

This Court should vacate the trial court's summary judgment order because that order was based on two errors. First, contrary to the trial court's holding, a county may be liable for its social worker's negligent supervision regardless of whether it violates a mandatory, statutory duty. Second, the trial court erred when it found the County immune from Jamal's negligence claim. The supervision and monitoring of Jamal did not involve "basic policy decisions" to which immunity may attach.

I. The Trial Court Erred In Granting Summary Judgment When It Found No Breach Of A Mandatory Duty Because Violation Of A Mandatory Duty Is Not A Prerequisite To A Derivative Liability Tort Claim.

The trial court erred because it incorrectly conflated two separate bases of liability, and granted summary judgment based on that mistake. The trial court held that where a social worker complies with its mandatory duties (e.g., "the statutorily required minimum number of face to face visits for a client receiving AFDC-FC payments"), there can be no negligence liability. (JA 901.) The County persuaded the court that it has "no common law liability for negligence [because] liability must be found on...."

At the beginning of the Argument Section to this Appellate Brief, the writer has provided a "Roadmap" for where the argument is going. The Roadmap previews the two main sections/arguments raised in the brief. Notice how the Roadmap begins with a clear topic sentence that is stated in the form of a conclusion ("This Court should vacate....").

The same is true for the first sentence following the Point Heading: a clear topic sentence that states a conclusion.

II. The Trial Court Erred When It Found The County Immune From Derivative Tort Liability For Its Social Worker's Negligent Supervision.

Once the County conceded it owed Jamal a general duty of care, to avoid derivative negligence liability the County had the burden to show that its social worker was entitled to immunity for its supervision decisions. But as discussed below, this was a showing the County did not, and could not, make.

A. A County Is Only Entitled To Immunity When Its Employees Make Basic Policy Decisions And Here The Social Worker Was Not Making Or Implementing Departmental Policy When Supervising Jamal.

The lower court erred when it granted the County immunity simply because it found no mandatory, statutory duty violation. In government negligence cases, such as this one, "'the rule is liability, immunity is the exception.'" (*Lopez v. Southern Cal. Rapid Transit Dist.* (1985) 40 Cal.3d 780, 792–93 [quoting *Ramos v. County of Madera* (1971) 4 Cal.3d 685, 692]; *Soliz v. Williams* (2d Dist. 1999) 74 Cal.App.4th 577, 584 [following *Lopez* holding]; *see also Milligan v. City of Laguna Beach* (1983) 34 Cal.3d 829, 832 fn.2 [noting the "basic axiom of tort law" that courts may not "casually decree governmental immunity"].

The second section of the Argument also begins with a short Roadmap of what is to come.

Under section A, after a topic sentence that states a conclusion, the writer begins a Rule Summary. Each statement of law is supported with a citation to binding authority.

Note the sentence length. The sentences are relatively short, and easy to follow.

Courts must narrowly construe immunity, for it can be "no greater than is required to give legislative and executive policymakers sufficient breathing space in which to perform their vital policymaking functions." (*Tarasoff v. Regents of the Univ. of Calif.* (1976) 17 Cal.3d 425, 445; *accord Doe 1 v. City of Murrieta* (2002) 102 Cal.App.4th 899, 912.) A narrow construction is desirable and "manifestly just" because granting immunity is "after all, a license to *harm*." (*Scott, supra*, 27 Cal.App.4th at p.144 [emphasis in original].)

Because of these concerns, only a limited set of cases entitles a County to immunity for its employee's negligence: those cases where the employee makes a "basic policy decision." (*Barner, supra*, 24 Cal.4th at pp. 684–85; *Johnson, supra*, 69 Cal.2d at p. 793.) Immunity does not attach to ministerial or operational decisions. (*Creason v. Department of Health Services* (1998) 18 Cal.4th 623, 633–34.) Only "peculiarly sensitive," planning-level activities that have "fundamental policy implications" or formulate policy are immunized. (*Caldwell, supra*, 10 Cal.4th at p. 981.) This is because only when separation of powers concerns are implicated—when a basic policy decision

The second paragraph is connected to the first paragraph with an explicit connector and a pointing word ("Because of these concerns….").

has been committed to a coordinate branch of government—is judicial interference "unseemly." (*Id.* at p. 981; *accord Johnson, supra,* 69 Cal.2d at pp. 793–94 [holding that immunity only extends to "those areas of quasi-legislative-policy-making which are sufficiently sensitive to justify a blanket rule that courts will not entertain a tort action...."].) To be entitled to immunity, therefore, a County must show that its employee made a *"deliberate and considered* policy decision[]" that consciously balanced risks and advantages. (*Caldwell, supra,* 10 Cal.4th at p. 981 [emphasis in original] [citing *Johnson, supra,* 69 Cal.2d at p. 795–96, fn.8].)

Application of these basic immunity principles condemns the trial court's decision. Social workers are not immune from negligent supervision claims because supervision of dependent children does not involve basic policy choices:

Decisions made with respect to the maintenance, care or supervision of ... a dependent child, or in connection with her placement in a particular home, may entail the....

* * * *

After a two-paragraph rule summary, the writer applies the law to the facts. This is an argument by definition. The writer also uses an echo link here to transition between the two sections ("Application of these basic immunity principles....").

This distinction between granting broad prosecutorial immunity for removal decisions from a family home, but no immunity for non-policy based, supervision decisions is a sound one. The government may only interfere with a families' or parents' right to raise their own child as they see fit in extreme circumstances: when the child is being abused or neglected. (*Santosky v. Kramer* (1982) 455 U.S. 745, 753; *In re Marilyn H.* (1993) 5 Cal.4th 295, 307.) The decision to remove a child from the parental home is not taken lightly. This is because the government is asserting itself to become the custodian of the dependent child. (*Id.*) Once the government acts, however, it assumes strict obligations to use due care to protect those dependent children under its care. (See *Lopez, supra,* 40 Cal.3d at p. 793 [finding that "subsequent ministerial actions taken in the implementation of" discretionary policy decisions are not immunized]; see also *Sava v. Fuller* (1967) 249 Cal.App.2d 281, 290 ["[O]nce the determination has been made that a service will be furnished and the service is undertaken, then public policy demands (except when the Legislature specifically decrees otherwise) that the government be held to the same standard of care as the law requires of its private citizens...."].) Social

In this last paragraph, the author makes a policy argument. Remember strong briefs often contain more than one type of legal argument (i.e., arguments by definition, arguments by analogy, and policy arguments).

workers can therefore not turn a blind eye, or ignore signs that placements are dangerous or inappropriate. (*Elton, supra*, 3 Cal.App.3d at p.1057; *Scott, supra*, 27 Cal.App.4th at p. 143.) If they do so unreasonably and the dependent child is injured, society—not the innocent child—must bear the costs of that negligence.

CONCLUSION

For the foregoing reasons, the trial court's order granting Defendant-Respondent the Los Angeles County Department of Children and Family Services' Motion for Summary Judgment should be vacated. This Court should remand the case for trial on Plaintiff-Appellant Jamal B.'s derivative negligence claim (the Fourth Cause of Action).

Dated: August 4, 2004

Respectfully submitted,

By_____

Austen L. Parrish

Attorney for *Amicus Curiae*
Public Counsel

The Conclusion is short and to-the-point. It does not summarize or restate the brief's arguments. Instead, it states the precise relief sought and ends.

Appendix C

Sample Memos and Letters

Sample Memorandum

The following are excerpts from a sample interoffice memo. The jurisdiction has been changed to the fictional state of Westmoreland.

MEMORANDUM

To: Senior Attorney
From: Junior Attorney
Date: August 23, 2006
Re: Paul v. Mary's Pie Shoppe—Evaluation of Mr. Paul's Claims File No. 13935

QUESTIONS PRESENTED

1. Whether Mary's Pie Shoppe breached its implied warranty of wholesomeness by serving a slice of apple pie containing a cherry pit to Conrad Paul, who bit down on the pit and broke his left molar.

2. Whether Mary's Pie Shoppe negligently prepared the apple pie by allowing a cherry pit to get into the apple pie when, while making pies, Mary's daughter removed the pits from the cherries close to a bowl containing apple slices for the apple pies.

BRIEF ANSWER

1. Mary's Pie Shoppe will probably be held liable for breaching its implied warranty of wholesomeness. Under the foreign-natural test, in which the existence of a foreign substance constitutes breach of the im-

Notice the Heading provides necessary information: (1) the intended recipient; (2) the writer; (3) the date; (4) the subject; and (5) a file number.

The first section is the Issue Statement, also known as a Question Presented. The Question Presented identifies the legal issue (did the Pie Shoppe breach its implied warranty) and describes key facts relevant to that issue. This memo uses a conventional format ("Whether....").

The Brief Answer directly follows the Questions Presented. The first sentence identifies the probable conclusion. Subsequent sentences concisely identify the most important facts supporting the conclusion.

plied warranty, the existence of a cherry pit in an apple pie is a breach of the implied warranty.

2. In addition, Mary's Pie Shoppe will probably be held liable for negligently preparing the apple pie that injured Conrad Paul. While the Pie Shoppe certainly exercised a high degree of care in hand-pitting the cherries for its cherry pies, a person skilled in culinary art would avoid placing the bowl of cherry pits near the bowl of apple slices.

STATEMENT OF FACTS

Conrad Paul has filed a complaint against Mary's Pie Shoppe after he broke his tooth while eating one of the Pie Shoppe's apple pies. His complaint alleges two counts. (Comp. ¶2–3). In Count I, Paul alleges that the Pie Shoppe breached its implied warranty of wholesomeness by serving an apple pie slice containing a cherry pit. (Comp. ¶4). Paul claims that he bit down on the pit and broke his left molar. *Id.* In Count II, Paul alleges that the Pie Shoppe breached its duty of due care by negligently allowing the cherry pit to get into the apple pie that he was served. (Comp. ¶ 15). In its answer, the Pie Shoppe has asserted as affirmative defenses that: (1) Paul's complaint fails to state facts upon which relief can be granted; and (2) a cherry pit is not a foreign substance when in a fruit pie. (Ans. ¶5–7).

The first paragraph of the Statement of Facts begins by summarizing the procedural background of the case. The paragraph identifies the parties and the key issues involved in the case. Notice how the very first sentence orients the reader to what the case is all about.

> This lawsuit arises from the alleged negligence of Mary Baker, the owner and operator of the Pie Shoppe. On the morning of May 13, 2006, Mary and her daughter, Daisy, made the fruit pies for the day. (Baker Depo. 25:5–8). The two worked side by side on a long counter. *Id.* Daisy pitted each cherry by hand. (*Id.* at 30:1–3). Even though pitting by hand is tedious and takes time, Mary and Daisy find it to be the only way to ensure that no cherry pits end up in the pies. (*Id.* at 13:20–24). After pitting each cherry, Daisy placed the cherries in one bowl and the pits into another bowl. (*Id.* at 5:12–26). While Daisy was pitting the cherries, Mary sliced apples, placing them in a bowl that was near the bowl of cherry pits. (*Id.* at 20:5–10). After all the cherries were pitted and all the apples sliced, Mary and Daisy put them into the pastry shells. (*Id.* at 10:11–12).
>
> That evening, Paul ordered a slice of apple pie at the Pie Shoppe. (Paul Depo. 45:2–7). After taking a bite of the pie, he bit down on something hard, heard a cracking, and felt severe pain. (*Id.* at 46:12–21). He spit out a cherry pit and a piece of his molar. (*Id.* at 35:1–2). Paul's dentist, Dr. Marie Currey, has verified that Paul broke his left molar by biting down on the cherry pit. (Currey Depo. 12:1–2). Neither Mary nor Daisy knows how the cherry pit got into the apple pie, but Mary speculates that since the cherry pit bowl and the apple slice bowl were close to each other, a pit may

After setting forth the procedural background, the Statement of Facts describes the underlying facts of the lawsuit. The description includes all relevant facts, significant to resolving the issues set out in the Questions Presented.

Often an interoffice memorandum will contain citations indicating the sources of the facts. This sample memo includes citations to: (1) the Complaint; (2) the Answer; (3) the depositions of Mary Baker, Conrad Paul, and Dr. Marie Currey.

have dropped into the bowl of apple slices. (Baker Depo. 89:4–6).

DISCUSSION

A court will likely find that the Pie Shoppe: (1) breached its implied warranty of wholesomeness; and (2) was negligent. In examining the claim for breach of the implied warranty, the court will apply the foreign-natural test. Under this test, Paul will have to prove that a cherry pit is a foreign substance when found in an apple pie. Paul will likely prevail on this claim.

In addressing the negligence claim, the court will likely apply what has become known as the skilled-cook rule. Paul will need to prove that the Pie Shoppe did not exercise the degree of care that a reasonably prudent person skilled in the culinary arts would exercise in making pies. As discussed below, Paul should be able to prove that Mary Baker did not act as a skilled cook would.

A. Implied Warranty of Wholesomeness—Count I

The court will likely find the Pie Shoppe liable for breaching the implied warranty of wholesomeness, when it served Paul an apple pie containing a cherry pit. In recognizing a claim for breach of the implied warranty of wholesomeness, the Westmoreland Supreme Court has adopted the foreign-natural test. *Frank v.*

The Discussion section opens with the likely conclusion and then an overview of the applicable law. The two paragraphs orient the reader to the analysis that follows, while summarizing the key components of the relevant law.

This opening paragraph on the implied warranty begins with a topic sentence stating the writer's probable conclusion. The paragraph then describes the general rule and cites to the leading case. Quotations are integrated into the text.

> *Captain's Table, Inc.*, 91 West. 60, 61 (1991). Under the foreign-natural test, a food preparer breaches the implied warranty of wholesomeness by serving food that contains a "substance foreign to the ingredients used in the preparation of the final product." *Id.* A food preparer, however, is not liable if "substances natural to the ingredients of the final product" are inadvertently left in the food served. *Id.* at 62.
>
> Here, the parties will most likely compare the facts of this case with those in *Frank*. In that case, the Westmoreland Supreme Court held that the defendant did not breach the implied warranty of wholesomeness when the plaintiff suffered mouth and jaw injuries caused when the plaintiff bit down on a cherry pit contained in a slice in of cherry pie. *Id.* at 63. The court reasoned that it is common knowledge that natural substances not intended to be included in a particular food are sometimes inadvertently included. *Id.* Concluding that a cherry pit is natural to a cherry pie, the court stated that the defendant did not breach the implied warranty of wholesomeness. *Id.*
>
> Unlike the plaintiff in *Frank*, Paul will likely prevail in his breach of warranty claim. Unlike in *Frank*, in which a cherry pit in a cherry pie caused injury, a cherry

The topic sentence transitions into a description of the leading case from the state. The holding is described by identifying the outcome and the key facts of the case. Then the paragraph describes the court's reasoning.

The topic sentence in the third paragraph transitions from the description of the precedent to an application of the law to the case. In this excerpt, the writer uses two techniques. First, the writer makes a concise argument by analogy. The writer compares the facts of this case to the facts of the case just described, distinguishing between the two. Second, the writer uses an argument by definition, explaining why pit is not a natural substance or an ingredient used in an apple pie. Mary Baker admitted as much in her deposition:

Q. Is a cherry pit an ingredient of apple pie?

A. Certainly not.

Q. Have you ever intentionally placed a cherry pit into one of your apple pies?

A. No, of course not. Why would I do that?

(Baker Depo. 54:3–7). The Pie Shoppe may characterize Paul's order broadly as a fruit pie, rather than a cherry pie, and argue that a cherry pit is a natural substance to a fruit pie. But the Pie Shoppe's argument will likely fall short. Paul did not order a slice of fruit pie; he ordered a cherry pie. (Paul Depo. 44:2–7; *see also* Baker Depo. 12:4–7).

B. Negligence — Count II

Even if the Pie Shoppe is not found liable for breach of the implied warranty, the court will likely find Mary Baker to have been negligent. For a defendant to be....

the elements for breach of the implied warranty are met (i.e., explaining why the cherry pit is not a natural substance or an ingredient of apple pie). It then makes and responds concisely to a potential counter-argument.

The memo continues. Notice how, after a clear heading, the topic sentence transitions to the next section.

Sample Letters

Example #1:

The following example demonstrates a standard format for legal letters.

YOUR LETTERHEAD
September 1, 2006

Via Facsimile & U.S. Mail

Mr. Ken James
7891 West Avenue
West City, CA 90005

    Re: *James v. ABC Corp.*: Possible Legal Action
          File No. 123456

Dear Mr. James:

    It was good speaking with you this morning. You asked me to assess your potential to recover from ABC Corp. in a lawsuit filed in California state court. In my opinion ...

[body of letter omitted]

I look forward to hearing from you.

          Sincerely,

          Jane Burke
JB/mgl
Enclosure
cc: Angela Johnson

The date, closing (i.e., "Sincerely"), and signature block is appropriately centered, while the paragraphs are indented. Space is left for a signature between the closing and the signature block. The sender/typist initials are followed by an indication that other things are enclosed with the letter. The letter also indicates a copy was sent.

Notice the formatting of the Opening Formalities: (1) the date; (2) method of transmission (fax and mail); (3) the recipient's name and address; and (4) a subject (or Re:) line. The subject line contains sufficient information to be useful.

This letter's opening uses an appropriate format: the salutation is followed by a colon; the introduction is indented and starts on a separate line; and the sentences are short and direct.

Of course, do not forget the basics:

- You should write legal correspondence on your firm's letterhead.

- As with other legal documents, you should use a formal, serifed font in a standard size when writing letters (12 point, Times New Roman is standard). You should avoid fonts like Courier and Arial, which are not serifed and less professional looking.

- You should avoid legalese or stock phrases (e.g., "Enclosed herein please find...."), and write in plain English.

- Your letters should end with a professional closing (e.g., Sincerely).

Example #2:

Example number two is an excerpt from a discovery meet-and-confer letter written to confirm an agreement between attorneys.

YOUR LETTERHEAD
September 1, 2006

Via Facsimile & U.S. Mail

John Smith
Smith & Kerns, LLP
1234 West Avenue
West City, CA 90005

    Re: ABC's Responses to XYZ's Interrogatory Requests

Dear John:

    This letter follows our telephone conversation from this morning, and confirms your agreement to amend your client's responses to plaintiff XYZ's First Set of Interrogatories. You have agreed to provide an amended response to the discovery requests by no later than September 15, 2006. I have set forth below what we discussed for each interrogatory request. If I have misunderstood our agreement in any way, please call me immediately.

A. Request Nos. 1, 4, and 5

    This morning you agreed to withdraw your objections and provide responses to interrogatory requests numbers 1, 4, and 5. In those requests, plaintiff XYZ asked defendant ABC to * * * *

This letter appropriately contains the Opening Formalities. Since the attorneys know each other, use of John Smith's first name in the salutation is appropriate.

The first paragraph succinctly states the letter's purpose. The audience for a meet-and-confer letter is primarily a judge. This letter includes details necessary for later motions (such as demonstrating that counsel for the parties spoke to one another by telephone, in addition to the letter).

The body of the letter sets forth the specific agreements reached. Notice how this letter uses headings to categorize the different agreements made. Each section also begins with a strong topic sentence that summarizes the key agreement.

Note that this letter utilizes the writing techniques described in this Handbook.

- The writer avoids legalese, and uses plain, direct language ("This letter follows....")

- The writer uses headings to separate the different topics discussed in the letter (i.e., "Request Nos. 1, 4, and 5").

- The writer utilizes echo links to connect sentences (e.g., "This morning ... to interrogatory requests numbers 1, 4 and 5. In *those requests*, plaintiff XYZ asked defendant ABC to....".

- The writer varied sentence length and used relatively short sentences. The sentence lengths are: 25, 19, 13, 13, 19.

Example #3:

The following is an excerpt from an opinion letter.

YOUR LETTERHEAD
September 1, 2006

Attorney-Client Privileged
Via Overnight Courier

Jane Smith
XYZ, Inc.
4321 Westmoreland Ave.
West City, CA 90005

Re: Possible Lawsuit—XYZ, Inc. v. ABC Corp.
(Trade Secret Misappropriation)

Dear Ms. Smith:

As you requested, I have reviewed whether XYZ, Inc. has a claim for trade secret misappropriation against ABC Corp. under California law, based on ABC's hiring of a former XYZ vice-president. My opinion is that XYZ has a likely claim because [summary of key facts or legal conclusion upon which opinion is based]. This opinion is based on the assumption that [set forth any applicable assumptions].

A. Summary of Facts

In addition to the usual opening formalities, this letter also contains an "attorney-client privileged" notation—critically important to have in any letter sent to a client.

Note how the introductory paragraph reiterates the client's question ("does XYZ have a claim for trade secret misappropriation") and then provides an immediate answer in summary form ("My opinion is...."). The introduction also sets forth the critical facts necessary for the opinion and the assumptions upon which the writer bases the opinion.

A. Summary of Facts

In reaching this opinion, I have relied on the following facts as I understand them. In January 2005.... [briefly describe facts relevant to the opinion]

B. Legal Analysis and Opinion

California law would probably recognize a claim for trade secret misappropriation under these circumstances. In California, trade secret.... [set forth the applicable law in a synthesized fashion, citing to key legal authority you rely on].

Based on this review of applicable California law, I conclude that a court would likely find.... [apply the law to the facts]

Using appropriate headings, the body of this opinion letter: (1) summarizes the key facts upon which the opinion relies; and (2) provides a legal analysis and opinion. This letter would go on to provide recommendations and advise a course of action, while setting forth appropriate limitations or caveats to the opinion.

Some reminders for opinion letters.

- Clients are paying for your opinion. You must provide the answer to their question. The answer should be at the start of the letter.

- The opinion letter must be well-organized and set forth the critical facts and legal analysis upon which the opinion is based. Using short headings — as with briefs — makes the letter easier to follow and understand.

- The opinion should be appropriately qualified. Although good lawyers will provide a recommendation or a suggested course of action, the lawyer will not provide any guarantee or overstate the certainty of the opinion (note: in this letter, the writer uses "probably" to qualify the opinion).

Example #4:

Example number four is an excerpt from a typical demand letter.

YOUR LETTERHEAD
September 1, 2006

Via Certified Mail

Deborah Green
Green Box Corp.
4567 Wilshire Ave.
Lake City, CA 90005

  Re: Demand for Payment

Dear Ms. Green:

    I represent Blue Supplies, Inc. This letter is to demand payment of $14,500 that Green Box Corp. owes my client.

    Until this year, Green Box always paid its invoices on time for products Blue Supplies shipped to Green Box. Starting in January, however, Green Box stopped making timely payments. In January, Blue Supplies shipped 400 crates of ... [recite the key facts upon which the demand is based].

    Green Box has failed to pay the amounts owing, despite a legal obligation to do so. Under California law.... [set forth legal reasons for demand].

The letter is sent by certified mail—a wise choice for a demand letter.

In the Introductory paragraph, the writer identifies who she represents and sets forth the specific demand. Even from a quick review, the reader knows what the letter is about.

Note how in the second and third paragraphs, the writer: (1) recites the critical facts upon which the demand is based; and (2) sets forth the legal reasons for the demand. Each paragraph begins with a clear topic sentence that identifies the paragraph's main point.

Under the circumstances, Blue Supplies demands that Green Box immediately pay the $14,500 owing to Blue Supplies. If Green Box has not made payment or I have not heard from you within ten days — by September 11, 2006 — Blue Supplies has instructed me to file a lawsuit. If legal action is taken, Blue Supplies will seek all appropriate legal relief, including damages and attorney fees. I trust this will be unnecessary, and I look forward to your timely response.

Sincerely,

Tera Jensen

TJ:mgl

In the last paragraph, the writer indicates: (1) the writer's expectations; (2) the consequences for noncompliance; and (3) sets a deadline for the recipient to comply.

Notice how the letter ends politely. The tone throughout is civil, yet firm in its demand.

This demand letter utilizes techniques described in this Handbook.

- The writer varies sentence length, but the sentences are relatively short. The sentence lengths are: 5, 15, 19, 10, 16, 17, 30, 18, and 14.

- The writer begins each paragraph with a topic sentence that captures the point of the paragraph — and each paragraph has only one point.

- The writer avoids using abbreviations, initialisms, or defined terms (e.g., Green Box Corp. = Green Box, and Blue Supplies, Inc. = Blue Supplies).

Index

References are to pages. Terms in italics are words or phrases that the text discusses.